Photographica

The Fascination with Classic Cameras

Brieftaschen - Kamera „Patrizia".

Photographica

The Fascination with Classic Cameras

Rudolf Hillebrand • Günther Kadlubek

4880 Lower Valley Road, Atglen, PA 19310 USA

12978078

Cover illustrations:
Front: Tiranti Summa Report plate and roll film camera, 1954; Argus C3 small viewfinder camera, 1940; Rollei 35 small viewfinder camera, 1966-71; Pignons Alpha 9d small SLR camera, 1965-69; Leica M4 small viewfinder camera, 1967-75; Noble Noblex Pro 6/150 F panoramic camera, 1993.
Back: Meopta Mikroma Stereo 1 green minicamera, 1962.

This book was originally published under the title *Photographica: Die Faszination klassischer Kameras [mit aktuellen Marktpreisen]*, by Battenberg Verlag, Munich, 1998.

Copyright © 2000 by Schiffer Publishing.
Library of Congress Catalog Number: 00-104363

Designed by Ian Robertson
Type set in Times/Times

Printed in China.
ISBN: 0-7643-1174-3

We are interested in hearing from authors with book ideas on related topics.

Published by Schiffer Publishing Ltd.
4880 Lower Valley Road
Atglen, PA 19310
Phone: (610) 593-1777
FAX: (610) 593-2002
E-mail: Schifferbk@aol.com.
Visit our web site at: www.schifferbooks.com
Please write for a free catalog.
This book may be purchased from the publisher.
Please include $3.95 postage.
Try your bookstore first.

In Europe, Schiffer books are distributed by:
Bushwood Books
6 Marksbury Avenue
Kew Gardens
Surrey TW9 4JF
England
Phone: 44 (0)208 392-8585
FAX: 44 (0)208 392-9876
E-mail: Bushwd@aol.com.
Free postage in the UK. Europe: air mail at cost.
Try your bookstore first.

Contents

Introduction to Collecting

Overview

It is difficult to portray this varied and fascinating collecting area briefly and yet thoroughly.

For one person it is simply a pleasure, a source of enjoyment, while for another it offers a wealth of insights into a more than 150-year-old history of technology, art, times, and commerce. In many cases, collecting photographica begins with a look at an old camera that brings back memories from one's childhood or youth—the Agfa or Zeiss-Ikon box, the Diax, Photavit, Regula or Paxette folding retina—or the astonishing discovery of an old shoe box in the attic, full of photos of one's ancestors in all shades of brown, snapshots that have survived many years. Of course, it is unlikely that anyone will collect everything over a long period, as the realm of photography is too broad for that—for the showcase as well as the pocketbook.

Thus some collect only photos, perhaps only old pictures, or certain subjects. Others are inspired by projectors and slides or their forerunners, the magic lanterns with their glass pictures. Still others collect cameras of the oddest types, or only photo literature, old photo advertising, and so on. There is really something here for everyone.

The first step to collecting for many: the rediscovery of early dreams that one could not afford earlier—whether the high-priced Diax, the little Photavit, or the simple Regula.

The Early History of Photography

It was in 1816 that Joseph Nicephore Niepce (March 7, 1765-July 5,1833) began to develop the process of photography. He was occupied with the technology of lithography, which had been invented at the end of the eighteenth century. The Camera obscura had already been known since about 1650. This at first served as an attraction in salons and at fairs, where one's own image could be seen upside down. A mirror was used to eliminate this problem, until painters, sketchers and papercutters discovered that the Camera obscura could be helpful to them. Now anyone, whether master or amateur, could draw without perspective problems. One needed only to copy the contours projected onto drawing paper or linen cloth.

That was the first major use of the Camera obscura. Many a lithographer or sketcher who may have lacked a talented hand used it to make usable, accurate drawings. In particular, the "poor man's portrait," the cut-paper or drawn silhouette, was in fashion at this time, since the possibility of taking photographs did not yet exist. Silhouettes can be regarded as forerunners of photographs, since they were likewise produced with the help of a camera. To be sure, the necessary chemical developments needed for true photography were still lacking. As can be seen from such silhouettes, the artists tried to add the shadowed contours of hair, lapels, and white shirts, even adding color to the picture. Handcrafting had to take the place of chemical processes.

An early forerunner of a slide projector, today a decorative collector's item: Laterna Magica, an oil-driven picture-caster for glass slides.

In what follows, we would like to introduce the history of photography and offer useful tips on various areas of this large and fascinating collecting field.

Carte-de-visite photos, such as were common around the turn of the twentieth century, are documents of the times and collector's items simultaneously. With a little luck, these interesting objects can still be found at flea markets for reasonable prices. The back is often almost as significant as the object itself.

Even then, conflicts of interest arose between painters or sketchers and the early representatives of photography. The "obscurists" were not regarded as genuine artists, simply because they began to make use of the technical developments.

They even made bigger devices, portable tents, in which the picture from above was turned by a mirror and cast horizontally onto a plate, onto which it was copied. Thanks to this mirror, the picture was no longer upside down. Was this where the invention of the mirror reflex camera began?

As a lithographer, Niepce already knew the Camera obscura, and surely made use of it. Perhaps he was also just a more easygoing type and asked himself how he could copy the contours. In the end there must have been a possibility of capturing, of fixing, this reflected picture. At first, though, there was the problem that this projected picture was sometimes unclear or could scarcely be seen at all. After several failed attempts, Niepce found a solution by using two black boxes, one extending far enough inside the other so that the picture became clear. This principle was later called the sliding box camera. Today we know that everything was just a question of focus, at least at this stage of the development. But Niepce went on experimenting. He put a microscope lens in the opening of the sliding box and was happy with the resulting clearer and brighter picture. This process was actually not his invention, as a hundred years before, in the first half of the eighteenth century, collecting lenses had already been added to the Camera obscura. Many historians even ascribe the basis of our present-day camera to Aristotle (4th century BC). Leonardo da Vinci is also mentioned in this matter, but we do not want to go back that far.

The slides for the magic lantern formed small series, generally with fairy tale themes, and thus were meant primarily for children.

Niepce improved the Camera obscura further, though, with a bellows that he attached to the lens panel, and developed an iris opening to improve image sharpness.

The next difficulties that arose for Niepce involved the chemical side of photography. How could he retain the image permanently inside this black box? Now we know that various experimenters, for very different reasons, had already invented partial solutions to such problems. In the days of mail coaches and slow exchange of information, however, they knew nothing of each other or the results of each other's work. In this way, they developed and researched in parallel time frames, without knowing of each other nor being able to exchange information or compare each other's results. Again and again, Niepce had to undertake many experiments without usable results. He achieved his first partial success by letting light touch paper immersed in silver chloride. In this way he obtained a negative of the image. Based on his lithographic work, he finally achieved success with a new series of experiments in which he covered a sheet-metal plate with a layer of asphalt and put it into his apparatus: after eight hours of light and subsequent treatment with lavender oil, the outline of the view from his window showed on the paper. He accomplished this in 1826.

At the same time, though with no knowledge of Niepce, Louis Jaques Mande Daguerre (November 18, 1787-July 12, 1851) was working on the same problems. Daguerre had to seek long and laboriously for solutions, however, before he attained his first success with a silver-iodine plate which served as a light-sensitive surface. The optician Charles Chevalier, who sold Camerae obscurae, finally introduced the two inventors to each other in 1826. From that time on they remained in constant contact with each other. In 1829 the two inventors signed a notarized contract which regulated the joint perfection of "heliography." Only four years later, in 1833, Niepce suddenly and unexpectedly died. After that his son Isidore took over the contract with Daguerre. The new company was called "Daguerre et I. Niepce" from then on.

At the time, the chief problems were seen not in what could be called the "hardware," for the camera was seen as thoroughly satisfactory. It was the "software" that caused the greatest problems: the permanent retention of the fleeting image, the improvement of its quality, and the shortening of exposure time from hours to minutes and seconds—or at least to periods of

Early photo advertising is a charming area of collecting and much can be found in early literature. Advertisements can be found in both photographic and general magazines.

Joseph Nicephore Niepce
(March 7, 1765-July 5, 1833)
He took the world's first known photo.

turned up everywhere. Every Daguerrotype was individual, for it could not be copied. Because of the long lighting period of about ten minutes, only landscape and building pictures were possible at first.

Then several improvements, both optical and chemical, quickly followed.

Professor Josef Petzval, an Austrian, developed a new lens. This was first built at that time by Voigtländer of Vienna. Later it was produced by numerous camera manufacturers, and it was still used in the "Photo-Ticket" of Turillon in 1907 and the "Petzval-Type" of Talbot's "Photokantone" in 1913.

It remained for William Henry Fox Talbot, an English scholar, to develop the negative-positive process, known as the "Kalotype" or "Talbotype," circa 1840. Now it was possible to make several copies from a single negative and even to illustrate books with glued-in pictures. In 1851, the Englishman Frederick Scott Archer introduced the glass plate as the collodium negative in the dry process, requiring shorter exposure times and thus allowing portrait photographs to be taken as well. The wet plate had to be coated by the pho-

time in which one could hold still in front of the camera.

Daguerre tried everything possible until, with the help of iodine and mercury, he achieved significantly shorter exposure times of only a few minutes. The image was fixed with natron sulphate. In 1827 he made his results public, but found no one who would finance and promote this new discovery. Fortunately, Daguerre had "connections with the highest levels," who were able to interest the Academy of Science in his work. As a result, he sold his discovery to the French government, which paid him a lifelong pension of 6000 Francs per year for it.

In 1839 the process was published by the Academy of Science, and was called "Daguerrotyping" from then on. This was the real birthdate of present day photography.

Daguerrotyping quickly became widespread, and photographs in frames soon

Niepce's first photo, taken in 1826. The well-known photo historian Helmut Gernsheim, since deceased, rediscovered it after many years of intensive and systematic research. The photo shows a view from Niepce's workroom window.

Silhouette pictures are forerunners of photographs. By adding details, artists tried to emphasize contours, hair, and clothing.

tographer a short time before the exposure and then developed immediately. With this process alone, photography definitely would not have spread to the extent that it was available to every amateur. But further possibilities were developed from it, such as the "Ambrotype," in which a glass nega-

The first photographs were named Daguerrotypes after their inventor. They were individual works that could not be copied. The importance they had in their day can be seen in the very elaborately made, velvet-lined frames.

tive was exposed from below and blackened on the back, whereby the negative appeared as a positive. This process would soon replace the Daguerrotype.

In the "Ferrotype," a metal plate was treated appropriately and thus produced a positive. This was especially widespread in so-called medallion photography and street photography, since the positive was available very quickly. But here the result was a single picture that could not be copied. In essence the Ferrotype, especially in its use for street photography, was a forerunner of modern Polaroid instant photography. But there were still various versions of the collodium wet process, in which the developed layer was completely released and transferred to another surface. The resulting "Pannotypes" are relatively hard to find today, since this process was used for only a short time and was also somewhat risky. For example, if black waxed cloth was used as the surface, the layer soon cracked and looked bad.

Using the same process, photos were also produced on porcelain surfaces. The wet layer was transferred to vases, plates, and medallions. This process gave very durable results and is still used to some extent today — even though the combination of individual chemicals and the gelatin used have been changed.

Naturally, the photographer of that time was happy to be able to show a photo after devoting a lot of time and effort to his work. Along with the chemical complexities and the amateurish equipment, there was above all a great limitation, in that the individual plate had to be put into the camera in the darkroom, a photo taken outside, and the whole apparatus brought back to the darkroom to change plates. Could this laborious method of photography have survived and prevailed to the present day?

The Frenchman Louis Jacques Mande Daguerre was the real inventor of photography. He made the process known to the public. The French government bought the invention from him and paid him a lifelong pension for it.

Twenty years later, in 1871, another Englishman, Richard Leach Maddox, brought photography back to its original course. He covered glass plates with a layer of gelatin that was light sensitive even in a dry state and could be developed later in a laboratory. With this, the chemical problems were solved and photography could be done by amateurs. At about the same time, the wooden plate case was developed, though it is not known by whom. Now the photographer no longer needed to take the whole apparatus into the darkroom. He could put plates into several cases, soon to become double-sided, and then use them in the camera in daylight where the pictures were to be taken. This was major progress!

This era also produced the so-called "salt-paper" photos, of which those who know say that they have a very particular glaze. Treating paper with a cooking-salt and silver-nitrate solution brought the copied picture directly to the paper and thus it also took on the structure of the paper. Later a layer of albumen was applied to the paper. In this way the picture could be seen directly on the outer layer.

Experiments with collodium layers on paper were undertaken until Johann Baptist Obernetter, of Perutz near Munich, was finally able to improve the process enough to begin factory production in 1867.

It is noteworthy that up to this point it was almost exclusively Englishmen and Frenchmen who worked to develop photography. Only the Austrians, Prof. Joseph Petzval and Peter Wilhelm Friedrich

An enormous step forward was the invention of the negative-positive process by the Englishman William Henry Fox Talbot. Through his "Kalotypes" or "Talbotypes," making as many copies as one wanted was finally possible.

Related to the wet collodium process was the "Ambrotype," which was also set in an elaborate frame and often colored by hand.

Voigtländer (who jointly developed the Petzval lens in 1840-41), can also be noted. Voigtländer settled in Braunschweig in 1894. German chemists and inventors were involved at that time chiefly in the development of chemicals, papers, and plate treatments.

Did you know that the Agfa universal developer "Rodinal" was first produced as early as 1891 and has been on the market ever since? After more than a century it is as good and as popular as ever. Further dates of German involvement in the development of photography are:

1840: Emil Busch of Rathenow produced lenses for Daguerrotype cameras.

At first the negative of the Kalotype was taken on light sensitive paper, so that in the positive the structure of the transparent paper can be seen.

1846: Founding of the Carl Zeiss firm in Jena.
1849: Founding of the Leitz firm in Wetzlar.
1850: Leonar produced photographic paper.
1854: Eduard Liesegang of Düsseldorf began to produce projectors, plus photographic paper as of 1857.
1860: Dr. Schleussner of Frankfurt (later ADOX) produced chemicals for the collodium process.
1862: Richard Hüttig made cameras in Berlin, in Dresden as of 1887 (later Zeiss Ikon).
1865: The firm of C. A. Steinheil of Munich (founded 1837) produced camera lenses.

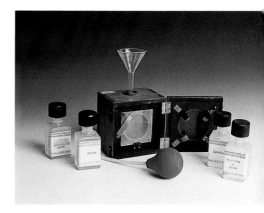

An early Daguerrotype camera with all its equipment, to be had today in original condition only for a four-figure sum. This replica was prepared by the late historian Rolf Oberländer.

1867: J. B. Obernetter, of Perutz near Munich, produced the first industrial barite paper.
1889: AGFA produced photographic development paper, and dry plates as of 1893.

1889: Founding of the Ernemann firm in Dresden; it produced and developed photo and film cameras.

1898: Mimosa of Cologne-Ehrenfeld, later Dresden and Kiel, produced photo chemicals and papers.

Let us spend a little more time on the chemical side of photographic development. The young bank clerk George Eastman was an amateur interested in photography and came into contact with the wet-plate process and all of its problems. It is thus no wonder that the new development of the dry plate interested him so much that he began to make his own. At first they only met his own needs, but he soon saw his professional future in this area. He developed a machine to coat glass plates and applied for a British patent for this invention. In 1880 he founded the "Eastman Dry Plate Company," which was successful. In search of improvements, Eastman regarded heavy, fragile glass plates as a particular hindrance. He continued to experiment with paper that was made transparent in an oil bath. He developed a roll holder, a paper-roll case which could be put into a camera instead of a flat plate. Despite the paper structure still being visible in the picture, many photographers used his rolls of film. The first "Kodak" camera was equipped with this "paper film" — but more on that later. The real breakthrough began with the use of rolled film, carried out by both Eastman and Hannibal Villiston Goodwin. Since Goodwin already had the applicable

It is said that salt pictures have a very special glaze. By treating the paper in a solution of salt and silver nitrate solution, the copied picture was transferred directly to the paper, which thus took on its structure.

patent rights, Eastman had to spend much money to buy the rights. With rolls of film, cameras could become smaller and lighter. Several pictures could be taken, one after another, without having to change plates every time. Then too, the film would not break. What was still lacking, however, was color in the picture. Many photographs, of course, had color added later, but that was not very effective and was also time-consuming and not very natural-looking. In the nineteenth century there was already much experimentation with regard to color. With the help of color filters, colored pictures were made of black and white slides. In 1907, the Lumiere brothers developed the autochrome process, in which colored particles were mixed into the coating, giving the finished picture a colored appearance.

Some examples of the many manufacturers of plates and papers in bygone days, such as Mimosa, Kraft & Steudel, and Voigtländer.

Naturally, these developments were seen then as tremendous progress, since color photography was as yet impossible. But the real breakthrough of color photography came in 1936, when Agfa came onto the market with its Agfacolor film — almost simultaneously with Kodak and its Kodachrome film. The original material, almost exclusively for slides, was followed by colored negative film somewhat later. The development of color paper was another matter.

Agfa was a pioneer and leader in color photography. Experiments began in 1912, and in 1916 three-color photography was already being worked on, while the Agfa color screen plate came on the market. In 1925 Agfa introduced the subtractively effective three-layer chemical film called "Agfacolor-Neu." Three layers of emulsion, separated by a color filter, were mounted on one coating carrier. The colors had great strength, since they formed pure pigment pictures, free of silver grains. As far as the chemical side of photogra-

Agfa ranks among those who led the way to modern color photography. This is a package of Agfa Ultra K color film negatives, in 6.5 x 9 cm size, produced in Wolfen.

phy, we are now up to the year 1936. But what had happened to the camera itself since Niepce and Daguerre?

Box and Bellows Cameras

The Camera obscura, with which Niepce and Daguerre made their experiments, was a box. The further development by Daguerre resulted in a sliding box, and William Henry Fox Talbot's first cameras were likewise boxes (called "mousetraps" by Talbot). Later, though, Talbot also used a sliding box with a lens and shutter. We shall meet the box again at two decisive points in the development of photography.

Kodak made rolls of film popular; in Germany, Agfa was among the early producers of the new film material, which brought much progress in terms of handiness (unbreakable!) as well as weight.

A new and completely different path was taken by the optician Peter Wilhelm Friedrich Voigtländer of Vienna, later Ritter (Knight) von Voigtländer, after he had produced the lens designed by Prof. Petzval. For this lens, Voigtländer developed a handy table camera made of brass; it looked like a World War II Panzerfaust (German bazooka) and took round pictures using the Daguerre principle. Along with the new shape, this lens was noteworthy for having four lenses in three elements, with a light strength of 3.7 — and all that as early as 1841! Voigtländer put this camera on the market in the same year. It was delivered in a wooden case, along with the chemicals needed for developing. About six hundred of these first all-metal cameras were built at that time, but only about ten of them have survived to be collected. For one of these desirable cameras, a collector could pay about $30,000 today — if he could find one at all. For the 200th anniversary of Voigtländer's birth, the Voigtländer firm of Braunschweig built 200 replicas of this camera in his instructional workshop; the cameras were not sold, but rather presented to selected Voigtländer representatives and guests of honor. Today one of these replicas would sell for about $1500; at a Cornwall auction one even attained a price of $2000. This form of camera was not adopted by other manufacturers. Only Romain Talbot of Berlin marketed similar looking cameras in 1913, but they were for dry plates. Their names, "Photokanone" and "Photogranate," have a military ring.

The first cameras had a problem in common: one had to take the whole camera to the darkroom, put in a plate, take a picture outside, go back to the darkroom, take out the plate, put in a new one, etc. ... Only the invention of the plate case, probably in Fox Talbot's circle, made the photographer somewhat more mobile and allowed several photos to be taken — such

A sensation in its day was the four-lens objective, first systematically developed by Petzval, with a light strength of 1:3.7. It was used in the illustrated metal Voigtländer camera, very rare today.

as on a trip — according to the number of cases taken along. The whole laboriousness of photography at that time forced the photographer to really "photograph" and not just "take snapshots." The one plate he took along, which involved much work before and after its use, had to be arranged carefully, brought into position, and taken care of — even though exposure and development depended extensively on personal experience and not on following specific directions from the manufacturer, using a light meter and standard chemicals. Along with the box, the wooden camera with a bellows became standard equipment in these "founding years" of photography. As studio cameras, these big, heavy devices, made for plates up to 30 x 40 centimeters and in some cases even bigger, were placed on equally stable, usually artistically turned standards or tables of adjustable height. During the exposure times, which at first were still rather long, the camera at least had to "stand still" because of its weight, while the person being photographed had to try to do the same before the lens for at least a few seconds.

At that time there were as yet no camera factories, but rather many camera carpenters, who built these wooden bellows cameras to order for photographers and photo dealers, but also to their own designs. The cameras were then completed by the owners with their chosen lenses. Shutters did not yet exist, and so exposure was done by the "lid-in-hand" method, with the seconds counted aloud. Sometimes cameras were similar, but usually no one camera resembled another. Since they bore no names or other markings at that time, they are very hard, if not impossible, for collectors to identify today.

Naturally, one wanted to be able to take a camera along to photograph a landscape or scenes from a trip. For this purpose, the camera (including its standard) had to be

A selection of the large-format cameras that were customary around the turn of the century (County Museum, Bitterfeld). They were made by camera carpenters, who seldom put their names on their products.

as light as possible. Thus travel cameras (called "field cameras" in Britain) came about, made of genuine mahogany, teak, or walnut, with a wooden front plate and sliding lens mount, matte panels or plate frames in back, and the bellows as a light-proof connection. In some of these models, focusing was done by moving the front plate, in others by moving the back panel. In the folding base there were several stopping points at intervals of about two centimeters, and fine focusing was done by moving the entire camera. Since the bellows folded, the front and back were pushed together and the base, being hinged, could also be folded up — a relatively handy camera could be transported. Efforts to decrease the weight continued over time, with the base and front plate no longer made of heavy solid wood, but only of a stable

A typical example of the traveling camera, fortunately fitted with a manufacturer's label (Emil Wünsche, Dresden). Exposure was done with these originally shutterless cameras by the "lid-in-hand" method.

frame. Naturally, a stand was also needed, for at that time nobody dared to dream of 1/50, let alone 1/100 of a second.

Today all of this may seem rather ponderous and laborious, but when you remember what a painter had to carry around with him at that time to paint a landscape, a field of flowers, or an avenue of trees, then photographers presumably had to deal with the same problems as painters.

Since we were just speaking of painters, they were divided into two camps by photography. One group feared being put out of business by photography, since the photographic picture was more exact than that done with the brush; the other saw photography as an aid in their work as painters and a new means of artistic expression. Some of them also painted the beautiful miniatures on the glass slides of the "magic lanterns," using them to tell whole stories. Children and adults alike enjoyed the first "slide shows."

A particularly lovely example of a Laterna magica, more reminiscent of an oil lamp — and that certain resemblance cannot be denied. In this model the series of pictures comes on a round disc.

Magic Lanterns

The concept of the magic lantern is that of a simple kind of image-caster. Does this simple explanation suffice? Surely, seen from the present day and with knowledge of slide projectors and their possibilities for multiprojection, they were just simple image-casters. But as seen by people of some 150 years ago and even earlier, using this device was an event — cinema, theater, and television all in one. The devices that were used then really were magic lanterns. In size and shape they almost equaled a middle-sized cookstove. The impression was even more pronounced since they had a smokestack on top for the resulting heat and inevitable steam. In those "pre-electric" days they were fitted with the customary source of light, first the candle, then the oil lamp, then the carbide lamp. How precious the magic lantern was to people can be seen in the relatively well-kept specimens that usually sell for between $75 and $200 at auctions today. You can find every possible and impossible design, and usually no one resembles another. When buying, you should take care that a few slides of the right size are included, for they were not yet standardized then.

These slides are painted pieces of glass as a rule, with the story being told in sequence. Fairy tales for children and adults were naturally popular then. But so were stories in the manner of the old balladeers, and instructional pictures from all over the world were shown and eagerly attended. Like pictures on strips of glass, those on round glass discs were common, and could be turned in the disc camera to bring one scene after another into the beam of light before the lens. At photo sales and auctions you can sometimes buy a set of such slides or discs for $50 to $75.

A variety of tricks were used to give the illusion of actual movement. For example, a windmill or its vanes would be projected into the actual picture, then immediately before or after, a turning one showing the windmill vanes. The windmill vane slide, mounted in front, could be turned with a crank, and the audience would be amazed by the moving picture. But the once so popular kaleidoscopes also had their colorful glass slides projected and given motion with the help of a crank.

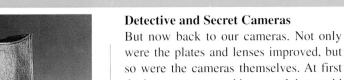

Detective and Secret Cameras

But now back to our cameras. Not only were the plates and lenses improved, but so were the cameras themselves. At first the lens was mounted in a panel that could be moved horizontally and vertically, so that any parallax could be corrected. In addition, the back panel as well as the base could be tilted. This allowed, in particular, adjustment in depth sharpness. We would like all of this in our present-day cameras, but it is only available in big, expensive specialty cameras.

Next, cameras were fitted with a shutter. Lenses and emulsions by then allowed such short exposures that they could no longer be attained with the "lid-in-hand" method. In 1894, Ottomar Anschütz attained 1/100 of a second with his slit shutter and could thus photograph a series of movements. The tripod thus became superfluous, for the camera could simply be held in one's hand. With improved emulsions and sharper lenses, the negative format and thus the camera itself became smaller and lighter. At the turn of the twentieth century, the standard format was 9 x 12 cm, later 6

A huge camera with a huge shutter — not in the lens, but in the back part of the camera. With this Mentor mirror reflex camera made by Goltz & Breutmann, pictures could be taken easily.

With the mobility of border strips, especially of slides, individual pictures could be shown at appropriate intervals and motion could be simulated — thus the magic lanterns became the forerunners and ancestors of slide projectors as well as motion-picture projectors. Can you imagine what fascination one of these shows would have afforded the people of those times? Try it sometime — but first turn off the television!

An especially well-kept plate camera made by Dr. Krügener, equipped with a red bellows and finely made mechanical parts.

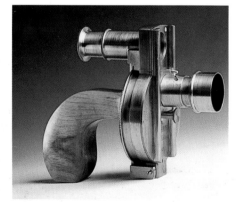

x 9 cm. Since copies were still being made, the negative was the same size as the positive.

A new concept arose: the "detective camera." And who would not have wanted such a secret detective camera? Aside from detectives, who had to learn photography to record evidence, the public demand was great. Who would not want to take surprising pictures and catch someone *in flagranti*? With the detective camera, the box regained importance. The intelligent detective cameras could be wrapped in paper and disguised as packages (complete with addresses), hidden under a hat or in a lady's purse, or built into a book or a briefcase. The great majority of detective cameras — and almost every camera producer built several of them — were simple wooden boxes with recessed lenses or magazine cameras that were loaded with six or twelve plates (and were quite heavy as a result). The plates were individually moved into position for exposure by an interior mechanism. The most commonly used system was that of the fall-plate magazine, which, activated from outside, let the chosen plate "fall" and released the next one. There were also changing-bag cameras in which plates were changed by means of a light-impervious changing bag.

The detective cameras gained popularity for a time from the exaggerated concept that a photographer always had to have a box camera on a tripod and his head un-

Various types of detective cameras: A Baedecker camera by Haake & Albers in the form of a pocket-size travel guidebook, the Lancaster Pocket-watch Camera, and the Thompson Revolver Camera by Briois of Paris. All extremely rare and only seen in museums or elite collections.

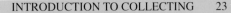

A magazine or detective camera by the "photographic manufacturer Eugen Loeber, Dresden." Hidden under a hat or tied up like a parcel, it could be used for photography unnoticed.

der a black cloth. At first the object was "more or less" sighted with the camera, but then came the built-in reflex viewfinder, such as was common in box cameras sixty years later.

Among the better "secret cameras" were "Krügener's Pocket-book Camera," various photo-revolver cameras shaped like handguns, buttonhole and necktie cameras, as well as cameras built into walking sticks. The cameras had meanwhile become so small that they could be placed inconspicuously almost anywhere.

Stereo Photography

Since striving for further improvement in photography went on constantly, efforts were made to give cameras spatial vision. The first attempt to achieve this consisted of making two exposures with one camera and separating them by the distance between a person's eyes. Two pictures were also taken one after the other with one camera, with only the lens moved sideways. Taking pictures simultaneously with two cameras was also tried. Finally, though, the stereo camera was developed, with two lenses separated by the average distance between two human eyes. Such a camera was built by Ninet of Paris as early as 1855. In the era after World War I, stereo cameras for plates and rolls of film were made by almost every manufacturer. The most commonly used formats were 6 x 13, 9 x 18 and 4.5 x 10.7 centimeters. Stereo cameras were made as sliding-box, folding-bellows, and spread-legged cameras. The typical type, though, especially in France, was the "Jumelle" camera. The front plate with the lenses was smaller and flatter than the sliding rear wall. The two were linked firmly

Stereoscopic human vision was not to be excluded from photography. An example is this Summum 6 x 13 cm camera of Leullier of Paris.

The most frequent representative of the stereo camera is the French Jumelle camera, easy to recognize by its pyramidal case.

by the pyramid-shaped case of wood or metal. In later years the interest in stereophotography died down. Only after World War II was there renewed interest, especially outside Germany. The Iloca-Witt-Stereo, the Edixa-Stereo by Wirgin, and the Boden-Stereo or Stereo-Colorist made by the Bodenseewerk of Überlingen were the best known examples of small stereo cameras, and many of them were exported, especially to the United States. To achieve the three-dimensional stereo effect,

the stereo camera alone was not enough. The results it gave were of two almost identical photos side by side. Only through a suitable stereo viewer could the two pictures be brought together and seen as one, thus achieving the view of a three-dimensional picture. One can, however, look at stereo pictures "provisionally" without any kind of special device by "squinting" at the pictures from a normal reading distance until the eyes bring the two pictures together to form one.

Stereo viewers were made in a variety of forms, from stereo glasses to a device that stood on a table or on its own legs. Stereo series of foreign lands, cities, and landscapes, as well as Grandpa's first pornographic photos, were very popular in stereo — and good prices are still paid for them at photo auctions and sales. Stereo cameras sell there for some $200, stereo viewers start at $15, and stereo projectors at $75, with many collectors paying much more for "cult objects." Today most current stereo cameras and projectors come from Russia. FED-Stereo and Sputnik can still be had at relatively modest prices. Those who are interested in stereo photography can contact the Deutsche Gesellschaft für Stereoskopie e.V., Kurt-Schumacher-Ring 50, D-63486 Bruchköbel, Germany. There one can get specific information about this area of photography.

Areas of Photography

Photography includes a broad spectrum of individual subject areas, so there is basically something for everyone who is interested in this type of collecting. Hardly anyone will be able to collect everything related to photography. Some people may combine two or more subjects in their collections, but most will specialize sooner or later. This may be for financial reasons, shortage of space to store or display the collection, or the desire to immerse oneself thoroughly in one area of the hobby. But which areas of the hobby are there? The whole realm of photography should first be divided into its main groups — and naturally, every named area can then be further divided into various specialties.

Collecting light meters is (as yet) far less popular than collecting cameras. And yet it is a broad area, starting with the simple calculating disc and going all the way to electric light meters.

- **Cameras:** wood, plates, small-picture, smallest-picture, stereo, certain manufacturers, boxes only, Leica only, Leica copies only, East German only, etc.
- **Camera Equipment:** flashes, light meters, film containers and cartridges, cases, etc.
- **Photos:** Daguerro-, Ambro- or Ferrotypes, stereo, slides, glass negatives, old albums, children's pictures, etc.
- **Magic Lanterns:** Devices, projectors, glass strips, slides, picture discs, etc.
- **Literature, Advertising:** books, pamphlets, ads, placards, trademarks, photo stamps, photo stock, etc.
- **Curiosa:** Photo figures, miniature cameras, Donald Duck cameras, photo lighters, etc.

There are countless possibilities, but personal choice and available space will determine the type of collection to be assembled.

Wooden cameras as an area of collecting: historically interesting and decorative as well, as this lovely British Sanderson shows.

Types, Carte-de-Visites, and Snapshots

Curiosities, called "Fotonippes" in Germany, are without doubt a growing area of collecting. They begin with the simple and still reasonably priced portrayal of a photographer in a "snowball" and include a more modern figure of a garden dwarf with a camera around his neck.

Probably the least amount of space is required for a collection of old and new photos. Who first began to collect Daguerro-, Kalo-, Ambro- and Pannotypes is not known for sure. At first they were surely mementos within the family, which were kept because the parents or grandparents were depicted in them — or perhaps oneself as a child. Looking at the dignified faces in these pictures today, you can well imagine that the descendants were proud of these pictures and liked to show them to others. It is quite likely that the spread of photography can be attributed more than anything else to the vanity of our great-great-grandfathers and grandmothers. Everyone wanted to see his family photographed — and thus made immortal.

How important and valuable these Daguerrotypes, Kalotypes and Ambrotypes were to our ancestors can be seen by the expensive and lavishly decorated frames in which these photos were displayed. In the period between Daguerre's inventions and World War I, when glass plate negatives, unlimited in number and size, made many copies possible, it is likely that many people thought of the old photos, each of which was unique. Breaking up housekeeping resulted in finding not only interesting furniture and utensils, but also an old photo album or box of old photos. Perhaps a Daguerrotype was even hung in the living room because it portrayed one's own grandfather. Since practically every personality type includes tendencies like "I have something that you don't have!" the uniqueness of the old photos was soon recognized as rarity. They were therefore collected, their values were determined, and a little later they were bought and sold.

Early photographs with their wonderfully decorated frames form their own collecting area as well as a relief from showcases of cameras.

Sometimes we find these pictures at photo auctions and sales in interesting cases and richly decorated frames. Since each of these early pictures is unique, one cannot offer value guidelines. As a starting point, here are results of the last Cornwall & Breker auctions in 1995, where the following approximate prices were attained:

$115 for an album with seven Daguerrotypes

$156 for a 7.5 x 9.5 cm Daguerrotype in a frame

$175 for a Ferrotype album with 75 photos

$240 for a colored 5.4 x 6.4 cm Daguerrotype with frame

$350 for a jewel-case of 16 Daguerro- and Ambrotypes

A complete Daguerrotype studio with two sliding-box cameras, standards, "headholders," Daguerrotypes, cases, frames and supplies was offered for $19,000 but found no takers. These old photographs naturally fall prey to time, and their condition varies extremely. If you do not already have experience with cleaning and preparing somewhat grimy photos, it would be better not to try it yourself. It is often said, "He would have done better to ask someone who knows how," and this is especially true of Daguerrotypes. Uwe Scheid, in his book *Collecting Photographica*, describes the cleaning and treatment of old Daguerrotypes. He rightly expresses a warning to keep one's hands off such undertakings. The seller's assurance to the buyer that "you need only clean them at home" is better ignored. Better to seek out an unharmed specimen and be sure that its condition satisfies you and fits into your collection.

Still affordable for the less affluent collector are visiting-card photos, found at reasonable prices even at flea markets.

Auctions and photo sales are often sources of very old photos from the days of the types. It is worthwhile to observe the treasures offered for sale and learn from them. Find out why one item is a Daguerro-, another an Ambro- and still another a Kalotype. You have already read something about them in this book, but from the specialists at a photo sale you can continue to expand your knowledge, making it even more specialized. As you go on to the next table, you will already be a little smarter and better able to decide whose wares are more suitable, and from whom you can best buy one or more old photos.

Along with the Types, you should also observe the "Visite" photos. More precisely, these are carte-de-visite photos. These are as big as a visiting card and portrayed a person or a small group. These carte-de-visite photos were generally taken with a multilensed camera, also known as a carte-de-visite camera, medallion or postage-stamp camera. Such cameras were used by professional and street photographers and had the advantage that, with four to fifteen lenses, many pictures could be taken on a large plate. Practical work was thus possible, as unnecessary travel, and thus time, could be saved before the plate was taken to the darkroom. There was an even more clever type of these cameras, in which only a single lens — even cheaper and more practical — was moved horizontally and vertically over the big plate; in this way individual pictures were made on the plate. Then too, only one plate needed to be developed and fixed. In addition, it was sufficient to prepare, develop, and fix one big copy. This was then cut up, resulting in small individual pictures — thus everyone had his or her own carte-de-visite photo.

Around the turn of the century, variously prepared copying papers were available. Here is an example of gaslight paper, its package itself a charming collector's item.

Such photos generally were placed in cases of thick cardboard and, grouped under and beside each other, formed whole pages in photo albums. Often the corners as well as the upper frames were rounded.

But not only the historical photos, produced by processes no longer customary today, are of interest and worth collecting. Early black-and-white (or sepia) photos from old family albums and attic trunks are very much in demand. The specialist or informed collector recognizes in these photos the paper, coatings, and chemicals that are no longer obtainable or no longer in use today. It is often said that the earlier products are richer in tone values and soft transitions. I cannot attest to that personally, and yet the old photos certainly have their own charm. In general, the available developers and fixatives were better for the paper used in their time, or for its coatings.

In this respect, it is interesting — and I only discovered this during the research for this book — that around the turn of the century separate papers were made for processing in oil or gas light. According to color sensitivity, papers were to be developed with a two-cylinder gas lamp, one cylinder of which was colored red. After that, the chemistry and coating had to be adjusted to the spectrum of electric light.

Cameras

STARTING AND BUILDING A COLLECTION

Collecting cameras is very simple. You buy a couple of Leicas, a Contax, and whatever else is pleasing, put them all in a showcase, and then look further. This would be one possibility, but certainly no collector began that way. Naturally, every present-day collector dreams of owning a few Leicas and a Contax, and rightfully so. One

can and should have dreams, but if they are fulfilled immediately, what else is there?

At the start, you can get a lot of pleasure at little expense, even without those jewels. Instead, for example, you can begin with a "Russian Leica" (Zorki C, Zorki 3, FED, or FED 3). They look just like a Leica. Of course they are not real Leicas, but they are good copies. You can also find joy with a Kiev 2 or 3, which were made on the original Contax production lines of Zeiss Ikon in Dresden. The assembly lines were disassembled after the war as part of German reparations and reassembled in Kiev. These cameras can be had for prices between $60 and $100. The $350 Leica, as well as the $250 Contax, can always be added later, without feeling that you've made a mistake by buying the FED, Zorki, or Kiev. Good copies make excellent additions to a collection of originals.

Above: One of the simplest and least expensive entries into camera collecting: Iso-Rapid cameras by Agfa can be found at flea markets at reasonable prices — and a whole series of variations can be assembled.

Below: It doesn't have to be a Leica — its copies are collectible too. The relatively low-priced Zorki can open the door to the broad spectrum of Soviet Russian cameras.

Sentimentality as impetus — thus it began for many. Suddenly you have the desire to own a camera that you either could not afford years ago or casually swapped for a supposedly better one — whether a Retina or a Box-Tengor.

Most collections probably came about when the owner lined up his or her own cameras from the last years or decades, which, thankfully, were neither given away nor traded in. At once personal memories are awakened — how difficult the choice was among the Retina, the Braun Paxette, the Iloca by Witt, the Photavit, or Diax. Further inquiries and phone calls to friends and relatives bring many forgotten items back into view: an Adox Polo, the parental Voigtländer VAG plate camera lying forgotten, an AGFA or Praktika that was replaced by a fully automatic Japanese model, or a Bilora-Box that someone simply forgot to throw away. It is remarkable what can turn up when you begin to ask and tell as many people as possible about a camera collection. The foundation for your own collection is already at hand. Still small but ready to be built up — and up to now it presumably cost nothing beyond a bouquet or a box of chocolates to express one's thanks. At first, of course, one accepts everything that is offered — this is quite correct. Specializing in certain brands, kinds, or types can come later, perhaps of necessity when the question of showing the collection arises and personal taste develops more strongly, or when the showcases and cabinets are full and some of the nicer specimens have to be packed in boxes and stored elsewhere. Only then must you decide on a collecting area, but that generally comes much later. At this point you can be happy to have a few cameras to sell off, so specimens for your true collecting area can then be purchased.

If you are ever faced with the decision of whether to expand or specialize, you can either call in an architect or sit down with your collection and calmly consider which collecting area is most interesting and which you can live without.

Possible collecting areas are numerous. For example:

•Box cameras
•Pocket cameras (110 film)
•Minox & Co. miniature cameras
•German cameras to 1945
•Postwar cameras since 1945

•East German cameras
•Single lens reflex or twin lens reflex
•Old wooden cameras
•Polaroid/instant cameras
•Japanese cameras
•Plate cameras
•Leicas and copies
•Specific brands
•From Agfa to Zeiss.

There are countless other areas imaginable for building up a collection. Some of those mentioned here will be expanded upon below.

BOX CAMERAS

One need not despise any "cheap" box or Instamatic camera. Who knows whether the odd-shaped Polaroids might not develop a charm as yet unnoticed? Perhaps along with the Kodak EK and Instamatic—if you know that tragic story.

The introduction of the Polaroid Land Camera in 1947 was a small sensation. Many believed then that this new photo system would completely replace negative photography, especially when color Polaroid came out in 1957. In 1976 Kodak put a parallel system on the market with its EK and Instamatic cameras, but they were too similar. Subsequently Polaroid won a tedious and expensive legal case that resulted in great financial losses for Kodak, as well as no-cost exchanges of all EK and Instamatic cameras for "regular" Kodaks. Since there were Polaroid copies only in Russia, and only one or two models of them (aside from two licensed products in Japan), here we have a manageable and, until future Polaroid developments, closed area of collecting that is attainable at modest prices.

Cheap boxes? No, by that I mean an interesting collecting area, if you delve a

At some point you must make a choice of what to specialize in so as not to run out of space. Box cameras, pocket cameras, and small mirror-reflex cameras are only three of the many possible collecting areas, which will vary according to your inclinations and finances.

bit into its background. Even if you rule out the first "The Kodak" (market price, about $3500), which was a box, you will find even a Replik (which was a replica made by Kodak of Britain in 1988) going for about $350. Besides, the original cameras by Niepce and Daguerre, and the models that followed them, were boxes. And almost all magazine cameras are not only boxes, but look like boxes as well.

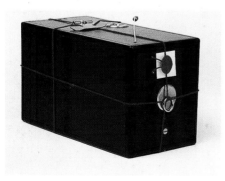

Still low-priced and almost inexhaustible: box cameras as a collecting area. From the simple (and not at all so common) Vredeborgh Regia-Box to the rare Merit-Box made of Bakelite, the collector has much to choose from.

A replica of the original Kodak box, the first roll-film camera. Even the replica brings about $350 today, and the original as much as $3500!

Look, for example, at the Baldur-Box by Zeiss Ikon, named after the then HJ "Reichsführer" Baldur von Schirach, who had these cameras awarded to HJ members for special achievements. This box exists in two forms, either costing some $40 to $50 among collectors. At Cornwall's 1994 autumn auction a collector paid $348 for such an item! He did so not only because the box was in good condition and an original pamphlet from the Third Reich went with it, but also because two or three other bidders were present and did not want to give up. The counterpart to the Baldur-Box, incidentally, was the Balilla Box, made for the Italian national youth group, likewise made by Zeiss Ikon, and selling today for some $175.

AGFA had brought out the blue school-prize box, which was presented by the school ministry to students in higher schools as an award for special achievements. In 1932 the AGFA Preisbox came out, selling for four Mark coins that had to bear the A, G, F and A mint marks. By October 1932, 500,000 of these cameras had been sold! What was a bestseller then must now be bought for $50 to $60.

Kodak promoted its film sales with similar ideas. In the USA in 1930, on the occasion of a not very round Kodak anniversary, 500,000 (yes, half a million!) Kodak box cameras were given away to all children who were then 12 years old, having been born in 1918. In this way half a million more hobby photographers and potential customers were created. Most of them probably stuck with it. The additional film and paper sales of the Kodak firm probably amortized this action within half a year. Every few years, Kodak also produced special Boy Scout and Girl Scout box cameras in the USA and Britain, officially approved and recommended by the Boy Scouts! What scout would not have made it clear to his parents that this camera ab-

red, green, and blue brought variety to the box-camera business. Big flash reflectors were built in, so that the box looked like a press camera.

Six by nine centimeters on 120 film was a standard size for boxes, for in those days negatives were just copied and not enlarged. Thus the negative format equaled the photo format. Even so, along with 127 film, almost petite boxes came on the market, such as Kodak's "Hawkeye Ace" and Zeiss Ikon's "Baby Box." This is an area that is worthwhile becoming acquainted with.

Not yet particularly in demand, but perhaps a rewarding area for that reason: instant cameras. Kodak produced some in a few years of production, to say nothing of Polaroid.

solutely had to be part of his equipment? These Boy Scout and Girl Scout boxes sell today for between $100 and $200. Naturally, other US firms followed with such scout cameras, but they could not equal Kodak's success.

If you go farther with box cameras, it soon becomes evident that they are not merely black boxes. The manufacturers tried to make their boxes as attractive as possible. Colors like beige, brown, gray,

Boxes, mostly for 120 roll film and 6 x 9 or 6 x 6 formats, were also made for 127 roll film, such as the Baby Box-Tengor by Zeiss Ikon.

A collecting area with an extension: original cameras and their "twins," such as this Agfamatic 4008 and the Pendants built by Agfa for Quelle stores under the trade name of "Revue."

MINIATURE CAMERAS

If you have a taste for miniature technology and perhaps dream of a Minox that is a few hundred dollars beyond you at the moment, you can find not only consolation but perhaps also joy in the little "Ritsch-Ratsch" Agfamatic by Agfa, the Pocket-Instamatic by Kodak, and the numerous dwarf types made by other firms. Not only Mamiya and Minolta, but many other brands of this type were on the market in Germany, including Wirgin's Exida 16, King's Regula 118, the Rollei 16, the Pentacon K 16, various Revue and Porst Minis for 100 film — fine and collectible pieces today. You can get some of them for between $15 and $40. The Edixa and the Rollei, on the other hand, cost close to $100. Holding a solid little Agfamatic or Edixa in your hands and operating it can give you a really good feeling and make minis an interesting collecting area. Anyone desiring to expand into this collecting area need only look at the many Japanese firms that simply miniaturized the shape of their big cameras for this small-size film, until these tiny functioning cameras could be carried on a key chain. Here the path from the camera to the so-called "curio" is not very long. In the sixties, Franz Brinkert marketed several miniatures that consisted of a normal camera lens on an lens plate. In this aluminum plate, some seven millimeters thick, both a shutter and a round film plate for six 8 x 10 mm photos are housed. The Enna-Objective Color-Ennit 2.8/20 assuredly promised good photo quality and was a forerunner of the later disc cameras.

To be sure, Stirn in Berlin had already used the same system of film discs around 1890 in its "Stirn's Vest Pocket" and "Stirn's Detektiv" cameras, as well as the Steinbeck A-B-C. Everything has already existed somewhere, sometime. These "efbe" cameras were probably built more for the collector than the photographer. At any rate, they are popular among collectors, who pay about $60 for them today. These and many similar items can enrich a collection of miniature cameras from the Matchbox to the Minox.

WOODEN CAMERAS

The other extreme is, of course, the lovely old wooden camera. The carefully built and finished pieces of carpentry work, camera and plate case, are most admirable in their own right. At that time camera carpentry was a special profession, producing cameras to meet the photographers' and dealers' orders. Their cameras truly possess everything that today's cameras lack but, in turn, have nothing that today's cameras have. (The exception: Studio cameras by Linhof, Sinar, Gandolfi, etc.)

These cameras had a wooden front panel with an opening, and on it a brass lens without a shutter; it could be slid horizontally and vertically on the lens panel. Today it might be called a "shift lens," and for the price you get two wooden collector cameras. With the accordion bellows and the adjustment of the camera vis-à-vis the object, photo size and sharpness were set, checked again on the matte panel, the case with the plate was slid in, and the photographer whispered a prayer and hoped for a good picture — often one for which a photograph collector will pay just as much today as for a painting by an old master.

Everything was in black and white — no, not exactly, for a close look at the photos shows soft brown tones that cannot be attained with present-day equipment. And the development techniques of those times are taught today only at masters' schools. The sizes were 13 x 18, 18 x 24, or 24 x 30 centimeters and even bigger. The 9 x 12 size was regarded as a small picture. Enlargement was not yet done then; the plate was copied full size in daylight — and for minutes!

The cameras were generally made of fine hardwood; mahogany, teak and walnut were preferred. Brass or nickel pieces, as decorated as possible, completed the elegant appearance. There were salon and studio cameras. If they were handy enough for one person to carry alone, then they were called travel cameras and could be folded up. In addition, of course, one had to take plates and cases along. In any case, a wooden standard was part of the equipment — a must in a collection of old wooden cameras.

The dream of every collector of fine wooden cameras — and yes, one is allowed to dream. This perfect replica of an 1860 Dubroni camera matches the original in every detail.

Today you would pay between $200 and $400 for such a camera, depending on condition and brand. For some cameras of this type the same model was also made as a so-called "tropic camera," made of teak or mahogany, generally without leather. For these, you must often pay double the aforementioned price today.

In some cases the manufacturer cannot be determined (see camera carpenters), since the names of cameras and manufacturers did not create images automatically then as they do today.

DETECTIVE AND SECRET CAMERAS

Even the so-called "detective cameras" or "secret cameras" of those days could not really be hidden. They consisted, in fact, of heavy wooden cases twice as big as a shoe box. Being magazine cameras, their weight was increased by usually twelve or twenty-four glass plates, which likewise had to be transported.

They were called detective cameras only because, thanks to improved emulsions and lenses, they required shorter exposure times, needed no standard, and usually had genuine shutters of the most varied designs — and also because they were really used by detectives.

The photographer's scene at that time included a tripod and a black cloth — with these two things, a photographer was not "in sight." Rather he was "secret," hidden behind a wooden box. Besides, many people just wanted to play detective.

A camera can hardly be miniaturized beyond the size of the Steineck A-B-C, which was worn like a wristwatch and made photographs on a tiny disc of film.

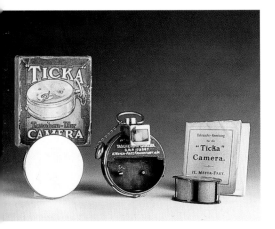

Another form of secret camera was made in the same shape and size as pocket watches of the time: the Ticka-Taschenuhr Camera.

Cameras hidden inside a parcel with an opening for the lens, or in the form of a lady's purse (Certos "Pompadour"), were also popular, as well as being a lot more sensible. When cameras later became even smaller, they could be built into walking-stick handles, hats, or ties. Thus the concealment was perfect and they really deserved their name.

In the fifties, minicameras were built into cigarette boxes (Marlboro), lighters, matchboxes, transistor radios, and fountain pens. Although some of these cameras were really made as secret or espionage devices, they can also be regarded as experiments into what could be achieved as far as miniaturization. The Walter Kunik firm of Frankfurt specialized in such types after World War II. Among others, photofountain pens, makeup kits and lighters were made and sold. Today collectors often pay more than $500 for these items. Each individual has to decide for himself to what extent such a price is justified.

The Minox has made a name for itself as an espionage camera since 1938, based on both its optical and mechanical qualities. The Kodak Matchbox can be viewed as a counterpart to the Minox. Although it was not made until 1944, it now sells for some $600. But all that came much later, when only collectors, and not photographers, talked of "detective cameras."

THE LAST AMATEUR PLATE CAMERAS

The wish for more easily portable cameras, and especially the desire to sell such cameras not only to the few professional photographers but to amateurs as well, resulted in smaller and lighter cameras. The folding camera with its conical folding bellows, made of thinner, lighter wood, equipped with leather and a Newton as well as a "jewel viewfinder" became the standard. The plate sizes varied from 9 x 12 to 10 x 15 and 13 x 18 centimeters. With assembly-line factory production, the devices could be priced more reasonably and thus interest more people in photography.

The leading manufacturers were Voigtländers (Avus, VAG and Bergheil), Nagel, Ica, Hüttig, Wünsche, Ernemann, Rietzschel, and Agfa. Even such names as Schlessicky & Strohlen of Leipzig, Schmitz & Thienemann of Tharandt, and Eusebius Schiffmacher of Munich were already impressive at that time. The cameras grew progressively lighter. Now sheet metal was

A typical example of the 9 x 12 plate camera is this Contessa-Nettel Taxo, with simple optics but also with the possibility of moving ("shifting") the lens around to correct perspective parallax.

also being used for boxes and lens carriers.

The popular tropic versions of the various models, which will cost the collector $200 to $400 today (three to five times the price of the normal version), were not made with leather, but rather in the old style, of massive teak, mahogany, or walnut.

These cameras also form an interesting and extensive collecting area. Here you can obtain cameras, depending on condition and brand, in a price range between $50 and $200. As for the condition, you have to draw lines, since time, war, and especially the decades-long break between active use of the camera and its rediscovery as a collector's item will have done some harm to most pieces.

Admirers of photography should strike up a closer acquaintance with these last amateur plate cameras. They are the last "mass" cameras, with potential and technology that can now be obtained only in professional cameras — and for a lot of money.

Many of these old cameras have horizontally and vertically adjustable lens carriers. Thus the result on the matte disc could be observed easily, parallax could be corrected when photographing, and the best degree of sharpness for the picture could be attained. Today this process is called "shifting." This is not possible, however, with any of the amateur cameras. With it, one could really photograph a house as a cube; with present-day cameras it sometimes looks more like a trapezoid. The

depth of field (this concept is debatable) could often be increased or decreased to achieve remarkable photos.

For $40 to $50 you can buy one of these old cameras today. They can be displayed in a showcase or you can have a lot of fun experimenting with them. No plates are needed, as flat film works fine and is safer. Suitable roll-film adapters, with which ordinary B2 roll film can be used, are even better. Color reversal paper (formerly Cibachrome) in the case in place of plates or film is very good for experimenting. The result is then practically a direct photo without a negative, and quite unique — almost as in Daguerre's time.

EARLY ROLL-FILM CAMERAS

This generation of cameras, from the twenties, completed the smooth transition from the plate to the roll of film, with all its advantages. It was lighter, usually had eight to twelve exposures on one roll, and did not break. Some cameras could even be loaded with either plates or rolls of film. A roll-film case, which cost only a few dollars, made plate cameras usable with roll film.

The plate cameras had angular boxes, while the roll-film cameras — made for roll film — had rounded ends. The 6 x 9 centimeter size became the standard; it still allowed contact prints but could also be handled in enlargers, which were becoming more and more widespread. Some people "misused" their old plate cameras by rebuilding them into enlarging devices. This was relatively easy to do, and the results were just as good as those of the other enlargers from this era.

The availability of roll film in place of plates brought new fans to amateur photography. With the greater number of exposures, the resulting lower cost, the lighter weight and compact dimensions, cameras like this Agfa Standard became popular.

Once they were common; today such simple consumer goods as empty film-pack cases are hard to find.

During this same period of the twenties, amateur photography really reached the masses. Film could now be put into the camera in daylight. The darkroom was no longer needed for photography, only for developing. Photography had become so simple that it could be done by anyone. Kodak, in the USA and Britain, plus AGFA in Europe and particularly Germany, were the manufacturers whom we can thank for the development and production of equipment and materials suitable for use by amateurs. Those who found it too difficult to calculate exposure, light, and distance simply took pictures with a box. Large numbers of the various types of cameras were not only made, but sold; many new brands appeared as well. These great quantities are still available to the collector — if they survived World War II — and at reasonable prices. For use with plate cameras, "film packs" came on the market at that time; they afforded the advantages of film but were more demanding to handle than roll film. Having such a film pack to fit a camera in one's collection would certainly be desirable. The acceptance of roll film brought further advantages.

A small negative size logically led to small cameras. One example is this French Dehel 4.5 x 6 cm by Demaria, made in the mid-thirties.

The wish for even smaller and lighter cameras led via 6 x 6 and 4.5 x 6 (still on 6 x 9 120 film) to 127 film in the thirties, with 3 x 4, 4 x 4 and 4 x 6.5 cm sizes, and to the present-day small picture size of 24 x 36 millimeters. Most film cameras of the twenties to the sixties were built for those three sizes.

By the turn of the century, Kodak had brought out fifteen different film sizes. After 1900, Kodak continued to market almost twenty more various film sizes for decades, making for confusion on the market. Kodak also built cameras for these film sizes, but their limited appeal kept them from catching on.

In the mid-twenties, perforated cinema film was used for miniature photo film, its size being 24 x 36 millimeters (plus other sizes). This has been accepted to the present day, particularly after World War II, thanks to improved emulsions, perfected optics, better film positions in cameras, and better enlargement of negatives. This development was particularly enhanced by the cameras of Leica and Contax.

A whole host of cameras from this era can be found on the collector's market, both bellows and rigid-case types. Almost all the manufacturers were active in this realm. Many postwar firms still preferred 127 film, and thus Agfa's Isoly, Braun's Paxette, various Kodaks, Biloras, the Zeiss Baby-Box, and many other 127 cameras can be had at prices from $15 to $50.

OTHER POSSIBLE COLLECTING AREAS

It is difficult to recommend a particular collecting area, for each person sees cameras with his own, and therefore different, eyes.

While one person may consider only the jewels like Leica, Contax, Minox, and Rollei good enough, another can find pleasure in the little minis built for 110 film by Agfa and Kodak, as well as by Wirgin, Mamiya, and Minolta. Still another may care only for the SLR or TLR, or be inspired by small cameras with fine mechanisms, such as Altix, Paxette, Retina, Vito, Exa, Iloca, Diax, or Photavit. Personal preference should always be the decision-making factor in the end.

Therefore, I do not wish to make recommendations in this book, rather to offer ideas and suggestions that will help you decide for yourself.

Other possible self-contained areas might be:

• Box cameras or disc cameras, of whatever brand
• Minis for 110 film (they are still around, but representative new cameras need not be added)
• East German cameras, such as Ihagee-Exakta, Praktica, Pentacon, Zeiss-Jena, Zeiss Ikon, K.W. Kamera-Werkstätten, Certo, Woldemar Beier, Pouva, Welta, Korelle, Richter Tharandt, Belca, Altissa, etc., or just some of these firms.
• West German brands with complete, often short but interesting firm histories, such as Balda, Bilora, Dacora, Iloca, Diax, Leidolf, Wirgin, Regula, Aka, Futura, Saraber-Finetta, Mec, Kodak-Stuttgart or Agfa-Munich

If you start running out of space, specializing or limiting your collection may become necessary. Those who have begun by collecting East German cameras in general, for example, might start to specialize in just one brand, such as Belca.

Let as look at the subject of Agfa. In 1925 the Rietzschel firm of Munich was taken over, and its products were at first sold under the new firm's name of Agfa. Although the firm was especially active in producing film, papers, and photo chemicals, they also produced cameras of all kinds and sizes, from the simple box to the SLR. In addition, Agfa's technical development continued, even though it is rarely mentioned today. As early as 1956 Agfa built the world's first fully automatic camera, the Agfa Automatic 66, a 6 x 6 roll-film camera that cost some $1000 at the time.

In 1959 the Agfa Optima appeared, the first small camera with automatic flash and so-called "magic touch," and progress continued. With over 700 camera models of all kinds, Agfa is an interesting collecting area, especially for those who love discoveries and surprises. For example, the same Iso-Rapid I can be found with its release above or in front by the shutter. A great number of Silette variations can also lead to new discoveries, not all of which are fully registered. The advantage for the collector is that Agfa cameras are still very

Above: Among the Kodak cameras produced in America the Medalist is doubtless a highlight.

Below: Compared to most Kodak cameras from the USA or Britain, those made in Stuttgart feature better workmanship and finer finish — like the Retina, Retinette and Retina Reflex. A Retinette I F is shown here.

undervalued and thus reasonably priced, but at some point camera fans are bound to discover them.

Kodak of Stuttgart is another secret tip. While Kodak was known for its mass production in the USA (even though a jewel like the Kodak Ektra of 1941 can be found among them), "Kodak Germany" of Stuttgart was responsible for the fine cameras. The Retina, Retinette, and Retina Reflex are cameras still regarded as "genuine German quality products." Most of these cameras are still in top condition even

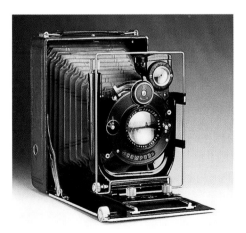

A superb piece for a well-developed Agfa collection — the Isolar 408 Luxus with brown leather. This camera is guaranteed to stand out among the typical black cameras.

today, since they were probably handled very carefully, prized, and carefully used. Compare an American or British Instamatic with an Instamatic 250 or 500 made in Stuttgart. Just touching it is sufficient. While Kodak of America used product designations that are hard to make sense of, Kodak of Stuttgart is understandable and orderly. And the Kodak cameras made in Germany can still be had for relatively moderate prices.

Those who want to do great things can specialize, for example, in Kodak International, with a total of some 800 models, or in Zeiss Ikon, with about half that number. One can also collect Zeiss Ikon with all its original firm names, which were later merged into Zeiss Ikon, including Zeiss, Hüttig, Wünsche, Dr. Krügener, ICA, Zulauf, Ernemann, Goera and Contessa. With the combination of over 1000 models, you could have a lifetime career. You must be able to tell the cameras apart very well, for Zeiss, Hüttig, Wünsche, and Dr. Krügener cameras were later sold under the ICA name as well, and some of them, like ICA, Ernemann, Goerz and Contessa, were later labeled Zeiss Ikon.

Why should a collector choose areas like Porst or Revue? Here, cameras of all kinds and many producers can be found. Then too, behind each of these cameras is a well-known brand name manufacturer that produced a "twin" of this camera under its own good name. It is very interesting to discover the counterpart, for none of them willingly admits to its "paternity." They are not copies, but rather "siblings" with different names.

CAMERA COPIES

Many copies and "look-alikes" of small cameras were built all over the world, particularly of the Leica, the Rolleiflex, and secondarily of the Contax. These copies appeared in the USA, Britain, Italy, Rus-

Why not this one? Porst, as a major producer, helped to make the photo hobby affordable in large circles for decades. Why should cameras like the Hapo 35 not be collected?

sia, and naturally Japan — even in East Germany. Since 1933, FED of the Soviet Union built its own Leica copies; the other copies followed after the war, when everyone thought they could copy the Leica, Rolleiflex, and Contax, top-line products of destroyed Germany, and repeat their success. There are even two books that have been written about Leica copies. One of these lists 100 Leica copies, the other 300. These copies profited from Leica's good reputation in that they were of interest to Leica collectors. For example, the "China-Leica" sells for some $2500 when it can be found at all.

In Russia, as already noted, the FED 1 imitated the Leica as early as 1933, and further FED models followed. After the war, Krasnogorsk brought out the Zorki, Zorki C (S), Zorki 3, and so on. These too were 100 per cent Leica copies.

The Kiev, Kiev 2, 3, and 4 are Contax copies (based on the Contax II and III, both with and without light meters). The prices are between $60 and $100. The special feature of the Contax copies from Kiev is that these cameras were produced on the original Zeiss Ikon assembly lines with the original machines. They were taken from Dresden to Kiev after World War II as part of the German reparations. So the fair question arises of whether or not these are copies.

The Kiev Arsenal has produced numerous copies. The Kiev 60 reproduced the Pentacon-Six, the Kiev 80 and 88 reproduced the Hasselblad 6x6-SLR, and the Kiev 35A reproduced the Minox 35 — although the machines and assembly lines of these postwar models could not be "requisitioned."

Even such a well-known firm as Canon (originally as Kwanon) began to make Leica copies in 1934. The Canon Hansa, the entire J, L, and V series, the various II, III, and IV types with their suffixed letters — all were Leica copies! In total, they add up to more than twenty models as of 1956, when the V series appeared as the firm's own further development of the Leica copies (which could be regarded then as modernized Leicas). Since both Canon and Leica collectors are interested in these first Canons, the prices naturally went up: for a Hansa one now pays some $4000, a J or S goes for $2500 to $3200. These cameras were not sold in Germany then and come from the USA and Japan today.

Nikon began in 1948 with Contax copies, with the unusual sizes of 24 x 32 mm in the Nikon I, and 24 x 34 mm in the M and S; only with the S2 was the standard small size of 24 x 36 mm used. The widespread rumor that Nikon had problems with the 24 x 32 size is nonsense, for the copied Contex took the exact 24 x 36 size. Despite this, the real reason is not known. It is possible that the company wanted to be clearly different, so as not to be seen as a Contax copy, or that they really thought they needed to create a new film size. But one thing is certain: the quality of the Canon and Nikon copies came much closer to that of the Leica and Contax than the copies from the Soviet Union, which had numerous problems. Did you know, for example, that Nikon supplied the lenses for the Canon Hansa? The Japanese firm of NICCA, which later became Yashica, likewise built Leica copies under the names of Nippon and Nicca; they were of good quality and are sought after today.

The good reputation enjoyed by the German camera industry at that time is not expressed not just by the many copies, but also in the names of the products: a Hansa by Canon, an Adler by Ricoh, a Doris by Tokyo Seiki, a Condor, etc. The situation changed over the years, though, until the Japanese manufacturers outstripped their former models in the seventies and began to dominate the market.

A perfect copy of the Leica self-adjusting camera with variable lens: Nicca III S with Nikkor 2.0/5 cm. Those who want to specialize in Leica copies will find a wide range — and need a stuffed billfold!

Even such presently renowned firms as Nikon started with copies, which they developed further with a lot of energy and know-how. The Nikon S2 is a good example, as it was well ahead of its time with its adjustable S36 motor, now very much in demand.

SMALL CAMERAS

Naturally, there are many small-size cameras and brands, some of which include interesting features of structure or design. The metal cameras of the fifties and sixties already attract a different sort of attention than the modern black plastic types. But it can also be quite an experience to hold a (plastic) "AGFA compact" in one's hand and use it. Not many know this camera or have already used it. It was on the market for a short time in 1980 and could offer more than the "compacts" of the time — and stand out above the usual models. The Agfa Optima in its various versions, the first fully automatic small camera, is an interesting collector's item, as it is still undervalued, and therefore available at moderate prices. Some East German cameras, such as the modern Zeiss Werra, the various Exakta-Praktica-Pentacon-SLR, etc., can still be had for reasonable prices, but the tendency is growing.

The Agfa Optima II is representative of the high-value mechanical small cameras that are still sold at moderate prices and are easy to obtain.

Camera Equipment

Among the less common but technically interesting cameras from East Germany is the Prakti II, which has a built-in motor winder.

How surprising it can be when, for example, four variations of one Silette model turn up that have not appeared in any catalog to date, or when the same Instamatic is found with a black or blue shutter button, the Iso Rapid I with the shutter control on top or on the front by the shutter. These are all interesting "twins" for a collection, and available for not much money. You need to find and compare these items, but that is what adds charm to collecting. The value is not always the most important factor.

Many small cameras, whether viewfinder or SLR types, are still low-priced today and available for under $50, so that a nice collection can be built up, to be enriched later with some gems when you "hit the jackpot." Basically, every purchase at a modest price is a good idea today, and perhaps also an investment — for in the world of historic cameras there will, over time, certainly not be more and more collectable items to be had, but rather fewer and fewer.

Not all collectors care about equipment; thus the many little gadgets that have been made for cameras can brighten up a collection. Range finders in their numerous guises are a good example.

Collecting camera equipment can also be very interesting and varied. Before and after World War II, many manufacturers produced range finders that could be plugged in. Thus an amateur using a camera without a built-in range finder could take sharp pictures. For this equipment you would usually pay some $15 to $25 nowadays.

Light meters are also part of this realm. It all began with simple illumination tables, which were already used in the nineteenth century and looked like calculator discs in the twenties. Chemical light meters in the form of pocket watches are now rarities, and appropriately expensive. Then came the simple optical light meters, in which a number indicated the amount of light that was still visible. At the end of the thirties, the selenium-cell light meter followed this principle, often with two areas of measurement and very reliable values. The firms of Agfa, Bertram, Gossen, Dorn, and Metrawatt, to name only a few, as well as brand names like Lunasix, Bewi-Super, Actino, Sixtomat Sixtar, Lucimeter, Ikophot, Photolux, and Metrastar will surely be found when you collect. The prices range from $10 to $50. At the end of the sixties, the more precise battery-operated CdS light meters were marketed by various firms; some are still on the market.

Above: In early times, providing the right lighting was a problem, as the lighting parameters of films and plates were narrower than today. Tables and calculating discs helped the amateur then; today these utensils are charming collectors' items.

Below: After calculating discs came optical light meters, which may not have worked very precisely but please today's collector. The design is always similar in principle, and yet there are enough external differences to make collecting them interesting.

Light meters were of particular importance at the time when few cameras were being made with built-in and coupled light meters. To this day, professionals and many serious amateurs work with these hand light meters. There are professional light meters that sell for several hundred dollars. For the collector, though, the "old" devices, from the table to the selenium device, are more interesting.

In a collection of camera accessories there is also a place for automatic triggers, which were screwed into the camera release and provided a specified time interval. Flash devices should also be present, from the old "lightning pan" for flash powder to the first bulbs and cylinders, the flash cubes, and the modern electronic flash devices.

For this very interesting collecting area there is as yet no catalog, although new accessories can be discovered almost every day.

Finally, here is an odd sort of tip: Does anyone yet collect camera cases? The manufacturers used to go to a lot of trouble to supply suitable carrying cases for their cameras, fitted to the shape of the camera and emblazoned with the manufacturer's name and sometimes the camera name as well. One can find the most varied and interesting shapes. Most camera collectors have several cartons full of camera cases, and at collectors' meets a dealer is happy when the buyer takes the case along with the camera instead of categorically buying "without case." Interested individuals could quickly assemble a collection without spending much money at all. One need only inquire about camera cases at collectors' meets and among collectors. In the end, a case is an original accessory for a specific camera. One would need only the space for this kind of collection.

Early flash equipment enriches a collection greatly, but can also be a collection area of its own. It stretches from rare capsule flashes over powder flash lamps and flashbulbs to early electronic flashes — and these things are harder to find than cameras themselves!

Related Areas of Photography

The collecting of cameras and photos is such an inclusive and extensive hobby that you can be completely wrapped up in it. Yet there are collectors for whom all that is not enough, and so collecting possibilities at the edges of photography have also been discovered.

For the history of photography, collections of placards, pamphlets, advertisements and trademarks with which the camera firms made themselves and their own products known in their own times an be extensive. This material can sometimes be found at photo meets and auctions, and often as well in the classified ads of collectors' journals. There, if you are lucky, you might find an old enamel sign from Agfa or Kodak for $75 to $100. As for brochures, advertisements, and other such items, it is mainly a question of the rarity value that the desired piece has for a certain collector. The prices can vary from $2.50 to over $50. The best place to gather such advertisements is from old magazines. That is not only less expensive, it also provides a better picture of the times and the other products that were advertised then, along with information that can make one take note, remember, or laugh.

Fun and laughter are summed up in the "various" or "curious" areas of collecting. Little garden dwarfs with cameras, Donald Duck cameras, trick cameras, little photographing figures and such are collected and bought for $10 to more than $50 apiece! In this area there is no limit to the imagination. Remarkably, the numbers of these collectors become ever greater. Even at serious camera auctions they can be found. More serious collecting areas at the fringe of photography are stamps and shares of stock. It is worthwhile to check with stamp dealers, as they will surely find in their catalogs some stamps from all over the world with motifs that concern the photo industry and its products. Such stamps were very common in the former East Germany, for example. At the Leipzig Autumn Fair of 1955 a stamp was issued that showed an

Early advertising signs of cardboard or enamel are very decorative collectors' items, and some of them change hands at breathtaking prices. They certainly expand the range of collecting.

Snoopy or a Practica hippo with a camera, a dogface camera or a toy camera that gives out pseudo-instant pictures — all of these are part of the wide field of photo novelties that keeps gaining popularity among collectors.

Exakta with a light shaft. In 1956 a whole series of stamps was issued, showing Ernst Abbe, Carl Zeiss, and the factories of the Zeiss works. For the 1959 Leipzig Spring Fair a narrow-film camera, a Penti, and an SLR were shown; for the 1965 Leipzig Autumn Fair a Praktica and a Pentacon Six, etc. As I write, the Estonian stamp showing a Minox is of special interest. From this very wide field I can list only a few examples; there is much more to be found. An advantage of this collecting area is that you need pay only a dollar or two for these stamps.

More expensive, exhausting, and difficult is the search for old stock shares from photo firms. Such stocks would be a big help in researching the histories of various firms. Here there are still things to discover. Many German photo firms were stock companies at some time during the course of their history. To date I have not been able to find any Agfa, Ernemann, or Zeiss Ikon shares among the document dealers I know. These things must exist, though. A good start can be made with a share from Kinax, the Soc. Francaise de Cinematographie et de Photographie, or an option certificate from Canon. These documents can be had for some $10 to $15. For old German photo shares, however, you will probably have to pay more. These collectors' items are, on the one hand, documents of their times that belong to the collecting area of photographica; at the same time, they are usually very decorative as well.

Photography on stamps — two collecting areas in one! Many countries have honored photography with images on stamps.

Many firms, such as Agfa in the example shown here, issued not only stock in former years, but also their own paper money. Since this was returned to the company and often destroyed, these documents are rarer than almost anything else.

The History of Photographic Firms

Not only the camera or the photo itself interests the true collector, so do their maker's chronology and historical annals. A series of good, readable books on the histories of various manufacturers and their products can be had. It would take up too much space to select and discuss individual books here, but suggestions are provided in the bibliography. Probably the leading specialist in photo literature is Lindemann's in Stuttgart; their advertisements can be found in photo journals. The publishing firms of Augustus in Augsburg and Wittig in Hückelhoven have already published valuable and informative photo books. If you request one of their catalogs, you will surely find something suitable for your collecting area.

At photo meets you can likewise obtain antiquarian and up-to-date literature at modest prices. Some photo dealers offer a representative selection.

It is fascinating to see how Kodak achieved worldwide fame in a short time with the right idea and, by absorbing its competitors, became the "yellow photo giant" in the USA. The offerings of the Kodak firm, a bit too varied in those days, reflect that situation, with the Bulls and Hawkeyes, Ponys, Brownies and Premos. In addition, you can read, for example, how Mr. Eastman visited Europe in hopes of achieving similar results, how he inquired of well-known German photo firms about mergers, in vain at first, but successful as of 1931 with the purchase of the Nagel firm of Stuttgart during the German economic crisis, or how seven British firms merged but could not avoid failure. In Germany too, the economic crises had their effect on the photo industry. In the crisis situation before World War I, for example, Zeiss, Hüttig, Wünsche, and Dr. Krügener merged to become ICA. This was the first merger of German camera manufacturers, but Ernemann felt stronger alone and did not join in. In 1912 the Swiss firm of Zulauf & Co. of Zurich joined the ICA.

An always rewarding source of photo literature is Lindemann's Bookstore in Stuttgart, which not only sends out its own extensive catalog, but also publishes books like these on brands such as Alpa and Voigtländer.

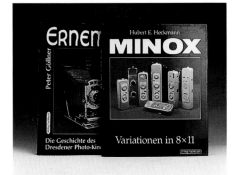

An example of a book on a particular brand, published by Wittig-Verlag of Hückelhoven, whose publications are very highly regarded among specialists.

The recession after World War I resulted in further mergers. The firms of ICA, Ernemann, Goerz and Contessa now formed the Zeiss Ikon AG. Although Kodak first wanted to take over the Goerz firm and made lucrative offers, Goerz finally decided to cooperate in the German union as part of Zeiss Ikon. A by-product of these mergers, of interest to collectors, is that Hüttig and Wünsche cameras were built at

A collecting chapter of its own is the early firm mergers. They resulted in the same models being sold for a time under two different brand names. Examples include ICA cameras, which also appear with the Zeiss Ikon brand name, or identical Rietzschel and Agfa cameras.

first with the ICA brand name, and later the same ICA cameras appeared under the name of Zeiss Ikon, with old model names but new trademarks. This area forms an exciting collecting subject, though extensive books on ICA and Zeiss Ikon that could describe these connections, give production dates of the cameras, and so on are still lacking.

In the realms of photo chemistry and photo paper, similar lines of development can be seen since the end of the nineteenth century. The later mergers of the I.G. Farben, as logical divisions of the tasks and production array, as well as the mergers through AGFA, came about for reasons of need or reason. But if we look at the period after 1945, several new camera manufacturers appeared in West Germany, only to disappear again after a few years, leaving us their histories and cameras. Examples include the Akarelle and Akarette of Apparate- and Kamerabau Friedrichshafen, the Bauer-Bosvch, the Bilora, the Photavit by Bolta, the Braun Paxette, the Dacora, Exida, Elco, Foinix, Mec, Finetta, Futura, Genos, Hensoldt, Iloca, Diax, Rollop, Montana, Luxette, Regula, Balda, Wenka, Navax, Wilca, Panta and so on. Who still knows the Bosch-Bauer RX1 and RX-2, very modern SLR types of 1980? Interesting stories could be written about every manufacturer.

In former East Germany the state-ordered equalization of 1959 led to a merger of Zeiss Ikon, Altissa, K.W. Kamerawerkstätten, Balda, Welta, Richter, Korelle, and Belca. The combination was then called VEB Kamera- und Kinowerke, and was soon renamed VEB Pentacon. This aspect is a noteworthy part of the history of the Dresden camera industry, which can be read in many books. This subject was treated very thoroughly and interestingly by Richard Hummel in his book

Richard Hummel

Geschichte · Technik · Fakten

SPIEGELREFLEXKAMERAS

aus Dresden

EDITION REINTZSCH

The former chief designer of the Ihagee Works (Exakta, Exa), Richard Hummel, has written a very thorough book on the *Spiegelreflexkameras of Dresden*, also treating the historical aspects of the various firms.

Spiegelreflexkameras aus Dresden. It is remarkable what further developments the Dresden camera makers were able to make, despite having to suffer severely from the dismantling of their factories and machines, which were taken to the Soviet Union. Their climb to worldwide importance, without help from the Marshall Plan, must

be acknowledged here. Another segment of the German photo industry's postwar history is the trade-name warfare between Zeiss Jena and Zeiss Oberkochen, Zeiss Ikon Dresden and Zeiss Ikon Stuttgart. The SLR developed during the war by Zeiss Ikon in Dresden (project name "Syntax") was built after the war in Dresden as the Contax S. This camera was the first SLR with a fixed prism.

It then became the Contax D, with and without VEB trademarks. After the fight for its rights between Zeiss Ikon Stuttgart and Jena, the same camera was sold for export under the name of Pentacon. In general, other East German SLR cameras intended for export were also given various names. These names often change from one export land to another. Thus the Practica FX sold as the "Kawenda" in the USA and the Porst Reflex FX at Porst, the Practica nova went on the market in Holland as the "Pentor." Many Practicas turned up in Quelle stores under the name of Revueflex, or outside Germany as the Jenaflex. The EXA was called Elbaflex in several export countries, etc. It can be very fascinating to trace these various names.

Personal tragedies also turn up in the stories of photo manufacturers, such as that of the American Charles Noble, who took over the camera factories of Guthe and Thorsch.

A dark chapter of German camera history concerned forced dispossessions in the Nazi era. The American Charles Noble, who took over a camera firm in Dresden in 1937, was such a victim of totalitarianism. He has built up the Noble firm again, and today it produces top-class panoramic cameras.

Guthe and Thorsch were both Jewish and had to emigrate for political reasons. Charles Noble, it is said, turned his photo-copying business in the USA over to them and took over their Dresden business in return. In 1939 Noble returned to the USA, but the camera business in Dresden continued to operate under his direction. The Praktiflex, which later became the Praktica, was his creation. When he returned to Dresden from the USA after the war to take over his company, Noble and his son were arrested by the Soviets (as Americans!) and sentenced to seven years in prison. His son had to do forced labor for fifteen years in the notorious Vorkuta work camp. The US government got him released before the fifteen years were up, but the company was taken over by the Soviets. John Noble, who possesses great determination and stub-

bornness, returned to Dresden in 1993 and since then has produced the exclusive Noblex panoramic camera for KB and roll film in his Noblex GmbH firm.

As another example, we can look at the Wirgin brothers of Wiesbaden, who, because of their Jewish origins, had to sell their camera firm to Adox in the Third Reich. They produced a series of Adox cameras in addition to the Edinex and Edixa cameras. They then emigrated to the USA. After the war, Dr. Max Wirgin stayed in the USA and became an importer for Exakta, while Henry Wirgin returned to Germany, resumed Wirgin-Edixa production again, and produced the outstanding Edixa-mat-Reflex as an SLR, the Edixa 16, Edixa Stereo, and others. This firm finally had to close because of the general crisis in the German camera industry in the seventies.

A last example of a tragic fate is that of Karl Foitzik of Upper Silesia, who was pushed westward by the war. He opened a repair shop in Lübeck, developed the business and built the Foica, Foitzika, and Unka (rarities today because of the small numbers made) there in 1948 and 1949. Even then they were known as "Lübeck Leicas." Their great similarities to Leica, especially the shutter, disturbed the Leitz works to the extent that Karl Foitzik had to stop production. In 1950 he built a small factory in Trier. Business developed so well that in 1954 a big new factory arose, in which not only cameras but also lenses were made. Most of the 100 employees had to be trained, for there were no skilled workers for the optical and camera industries in Trier. Sixty percent of production was intended for export. Just at this stage of upward development and business success, Karl Foitzik lost his life though a skid on the ice in December 1955.

The histories of camera firms have included not only misfortunes, but curious events as well. Where, for example, would you locate the firm of Neumann & Heilmann? In Germany? A major error, for this firm existed in Japan before World War II. There they built and marketed a 6 x 9 roll-film bellows camera by the name of Condor and also produced camera shutters. And what would you think of a firm named Nixon? This firm built the Ideal Color 35 and the Nixette in Wuppertal until it was taken over by Agfa and converted to the production of Agfa photo equipment.

It can be very informative to study the cameras, their manufacturers, and the whole related area. One learns not only the technology and possibilities of a given time, but also gains insight into further developments, mistakes, failures, and interruptions in development that culminate in success years later.

For only a few years, Karl Foitzik produced cameras, first in Lübeck, then in Trier. Models like the illustrated Foinix 35, the Foica, and the Unca are rare and sought after today.

Thus there is much to be discovered in connection with the collecting of cameras and photography. This activity can bring great joy and can fit any purse. You do not have to start with a Leica, but on the way to it you can find unusual and interesting items at low cost — and learn a lot in the process!

Opportunities to Buy

THE PHOTO DEALER
How do you go about looking for the cameras described above, once you've had success with the first harvest among relatives and friends and would like to go on collecting?

There are numerous photo dealers who stand out for their extensive, well-assorted stocks of collector cameras. Foto Gregor in Cologne is one of Germany's best sources in this realm.

One place to start is with a photo dealer who is known for his good supply of used cameras. There you have the advantage of being able to see and examine an extensive array. Even smaller dealers who sometimes take an old camera in trade can be interesting sources from which you can obtain many good buys.

Checking the shutter for long and short periods, film advance, and light-meter function, should be obligatory after examining the external condition. In some cameras the shutter functions properly only when the camera has film or a fresh battery in it. The external condition can be checked quickly, so that you can decide how the camera will look in the collection. Proper function and good condition (for really old cameras one must make allowances) are prerequisites for a decision to buy — if the price is right. To assess that, one should always have a pocket price guide on hand, in which pieces already in the collection have been checked off. Whether and how far you stray from the recommended value is up to each individual. Naturally, staying under the catalog price is always good, but a very special item may, at the moment of decision, be worth more to you. If you are ready to pay a high price, it can still be a good buy from your standpoint. If you immediately check the value in the price guide, you have no reason to be annoyed later at having paid too much for the camera.

PHOTO JOURNALS
Advertisements in photo journals, special collector publications (such as "PHOTO*Deal*" or "Photographica Cabinett," "CD-Aktuelle" of the Daguerre Club), and in advertising sheets are another source.

Classified ads in specialist journals are good sources. Such ads can be found in the quarterly photographica magazine "PHOTO*Deal*," in which many collector cameras are offered.

In many cases, though, you cannot see and test the camera right away. Instead you must trust the seller and his description. I can say from my own experience that all of my purchases to date have been fine (except for one case where the flap of the light meter lacked an Edixamat). Serious collectors also have the right to return a purchase within a week or surrender the deposit. In such a case the buyer should be kind enough to telephone, immediately after examining the camera, and either agree or state that he is returning it.

PHOTO MEETS AND AUCTIONS

Flea markets sometimes offer interesting items, usually neglected and often only in the lower price ranges, while photo meets (schedules usually announced in photo journals) offer a really inclusive array of all kinds of cameras and equipment. Here you can spot good pieces, examine them, compare prices, and make deals. At a photo meet you will also find dealers who are well-informed collectors, often specialists in their own collecting area, with whom you can "talk shop" pleasantly. There you can get answers to almost all the questions that arise about a camera or a collection.

Often, lasting contacts are made for the purpose of exchanging information and cameras. Here there are not only cameras but any kind of equipment that you can imagine, plus journals and old literature that can no longer be bought in the shops. Most photo meets offer such an interesting array that it is worthwhile driving a few hours now and then. If you have enough duplicates or cameras outside your collecting area to offer, you can rent a table at a photo meet yourself and offer your treasures for sale. But get in touch with the promoter promptly, for the tables are usually booked weeks in advance. One more tip for visit-

All over Germany there are more than one hundred photo meets, with everything involving cameras for sale. Most meets take place in big halls, but there are also open-air events, like the one known to insiders at Bievre near Paris.

At photographic auctions, such as those of the renowned Cologne auction house of Cornwall, a fine array of mostly high-value cameras can be found, some of them not available at all through other sources. Yet bargains can also be found at the auctions.

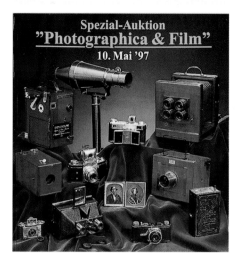

There are times when intensive searching at photo meets just will not fill the last holes in one's collection. Photographic auctions, the best-known being Cornwall and Auction-Team in Cologne and Christie's in London, are another possible source.

ing a photo meet: don't take more money than you want to spend that day. You will see that the allure is great. Always look for good collectible condition as well as a reasonable buying price.

As a source of cameras and photographic items, you should not forget auctions. Cornwall and Breker ("Auction-Team") in Cologne are probably the best-known. Each holds a spring and autumn auction every year. It would be nice if the two would schedule their auctions at different times and not on the same day. For collectors, who are their customers, that would obviously be desirable. Collectors

could then at least have the possibility attending both auctions.

Every collector should take part in one of these auctions at least once, to become acquainted with the atmosphere, the offerings, and the nature of the bidding at an auction house. But collectors can also go to Christie's in London, where several photo auctions are held every year. Be sure to order the auction catalog well in advance, as they are already mailed out weeks before the auction. The catalogs cost about $25. It is recommended that you mark the items that are of particular interest and write in a personal price limit. At the preview,

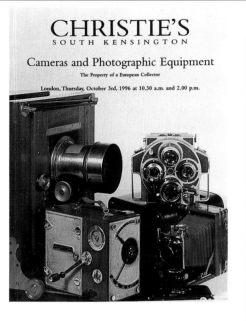

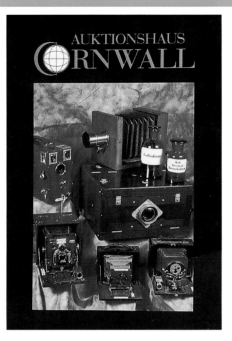

which is usually several days but at least an hour or two before the auction begins, you can examine interesting articles and sometimes even test them. Then, in the hectic tempo of the auction you will know how far you can afford to go and eliminate overly expensive purchases. This is especially important when several bidders try to outbid each other and acquire the desired piece no matter what — even at twice its worth. Sale prices at auctions have their own laws, or should we say their own lawlessness? When two or three bidders are really "hung up" on an object, the price can rise to dizzying heights. Thus it can happen that the price of a camera that started at $750 and has an actual value of some $1200 is bid up so high that it finally sells for $4500! This happens often when Japanese bidders place their bids by telephone and pay any price. On the other hand, you can get a good buy on a low-priced lot or an individual, moderately-priced camera, for the bidders at an auction usually come for the expensive cameras and are not interested in the lower-priced ones. Three good Retinas for $60 can actually be had, for example. Bear in mind too, that a fee of about 20% of the sale price has to be paid to the auction house.

Value and Condition of Collectors' Items

"The price of an old camera depends on the buyer's mood at the moment of purchase," an American author wrote. This statement is absolutely true.

It would be simpler if the price of a collector camera was dependent only on its age and the number of other cameras of the same type presently on the market. Another approach might be a calculation involving the camera's former selling price in relation to its age. Although that may sound logical, such a result does not represent reality. In fact, someone *has* published a list for used equipment in the photo trade. It includes a calculation table that determines the price of the camera when it was new, and relates it to an index of increased retail prices of all wares as well as an index of employees' salaries, based on the year the camera was made and the present situation! Read this sentence calmly one more time — really! It could scarcely be made more complicated or more unreal. I once tried to work out the price of a camera using these two index tables and know what chaos resulted.

Strictly speaking, only the collector determines the price. Thus, for example, cameras by Leica, Contax, Robot, Rollei and Minox are not so expensive because they are so old or so rare, but because there are many collectors ready to pay for these brands that they have chosen as their collecting area. There are many more Leicas than Contax on the market. Although both brands are "first-class cameras," you can buy a Contax for some $250, while for a Leica, depending on its type, you would have to pay some $500 or more. An Oga or Ogamatik by Obergassner, an Infra by Oehler, a Finetta by Saraber, a Luxette, and a Rollop are much rarer than a Rollei 35. But collectors pay some $250 for a Rollei, while the Infra may not sell at $60. An old Kodak does not become a "thing of value" just because it is more than sixty years old. This camera is available for $25. In this case there are more surviving specimens than interested buyers. As simple as the matter may sound, it is really quite complicated.

Even though the price of a Leica, Rollei, or Minox is very high, there is no use complaining as long as a collector pays it. For these brands the situation will presumably stay as it is for some time. You can avoid this difficulty, of course, by choosing a different collecting area — there are many other nice and interesting cameras.

Collecting classic cameras follows its own laws; the degree of rarity alone is not all there is to it. The Gewirette by Wirgin shown here, for example, is much rarer than most Leicas, but the latter are usually priced above the other brands.

Since the Iron Curtain has fallen and more cameras have come to Germany from the former Soviet Union, interest in these cameras has increased greatly. There are also several noteworthy models among them, like this Leningrad with spring motor.

Presently undervalued are, as noted, Agfa and cameras from the former East Germany and Soviet Union. Many people quickly got rid of their East German camera and bought a Japanese brand because it was "in" after the change, recognizing the value and excellent technology of these cameras only several years later. While Soviet cameras have really been dumped on the German market in the last three years, hardly any are following them now. In addition, more and more German collectors, inspired by the Leica and Contax copies, are getting interested in cameras from the former Soviet Union. All these factors influence the market price of a collector's or secondhand camera.

Here is another tip: very recently, "gilded" luxury Leicas have been offered for sale. These are reworked FEDs or Zorkis, with their original brand names ground off and "Leica" or "Leitz" engraved on them instead. All the metal parts are "brass-plated." Recently these objects have also been given a lens cover with the "Leitz" or "Leica" name on it. On many, the upper plate has also been engraved with the German eagle and "BILDBER-ICHTER." They have also been fitted with imitation lizard leather.

If these cameras were genuine, they would be worth some $22,500; as authentic transformations of a Leica into a luxury object, about $1900. This Russian version, reworked in Russia or Poland, is sold at flea markets for $140 to $150. Numerous collectors have called me, told me they made the "buy of their lives," and were rather disappointed after we talked. You can, of course, put one of these "falsifications" in a collection, but strictly as a falsification. One must know for sure that it is not a genuine Leica.

Collectors, like dealers, need an overview of the cameras on the market, their technical data, and their identifying and differentiating marks — and that means a camera collector's catalog. In order to provide collectors and dealers with at least a guidebook for orientation, I have taken note of advertisements in specialist journals, auction prices (with reservations), prices at photo meets, and in dealers' showcases for

Copies of the luxury Leicas — sometimes with imaginative engraving that Leicas never had — are often offered at photo shows and flea markets. Years ago, trusting collectors were fooled by them, but today they recognize the copies as such.

Kadlubeks Kamera-Katalog '97-98 lists the data and values of over 17,000 cameras, and depicts more than 2000 cameras. It is the most inclusive and detailed reference work in the German language.

a long time, compared them, and derived a value that corresponds to the price fluctuations on the present-day world market. This value is to be understood as a guideline. More than 17,000 models and more than 2000 illustrations are included in the 1997-98 edition of *Kadlubeks Kamera-Katalog* — exactly what the collector needs and did not have previously. In order to make it even easier for collectors, a pocket price

guide that is small and light enough to take along everywhere is included in the price of the book.

The condition or "degree of maintenance" of an item plays a role in setting the price as well. There are various systems of designating condition, from A to E, 1 to 10, 1 to 6, and so on. Some would rather consider appearance and technical functioning separately (which is not necessarily wrong), but recently the following evaluation system from A to E has prevailed in Germany:

A = as good as new, no signs of use, in original package if possible = 125% the catalog price.

B = very good condition, scarcely any signs of use = 100% the catalog price.

C = good condition, normal signs of use = 80% the catalog price.

D = poor condition, severe signs of use = 50% the catalog price.

E = poor condition, scarcely reparable, usable as a source of spare parts = no catalog price, junk price.

Normally, groups A and B belong in a really good collection, as well as C under special conditions. A category D camera should be in a collection only if you can repair it or improve its condition. Class E cameras are really of use only for spare parts, as are cameras with major defects.

Preserving and Cataloging

No general advice for the display of collector cameras can be offered, due to the variety of living conditions and individual situations. For example, do others in your home also enjoy these beautiful objects? Will there always be enough room for them in the living room? If not, you may have to ask yourself whether the basement, attic, or workroom will be the best place to keep the collection. Of course, you can keep a camera collection on bookshelves and dust it once a month, but after two or three years the pieces will no longer look very good. It is really preferable to house your collection in a showcase; there too, you will see dust on the glass plates two or three times a year but the cleaning required will do the cameras good.

A form like the one shown here can be used to list and catalog your collection. You should do this in two sections, one for the camera numbers and one for the lens numbers. This is necessary not only for the sake of your own information, but especially for the (hopefully never occurring) need to show the insurance company just which pieces were taken in a burglary, and to describe them thoroughly. Photos of the cameras are also helpful and important, not only of individual pieces but also of the whole collection. In this way the insurance company will have proof that all of these cameras were originally there in the showcase.

For your own information as well as for your safety in case of theft, a card file is a good idea — either with the help of illustrated cards like these or with a corresponding computer program.

Depending on the size and value of your collection, it is important to talk with your insurance agent and find out to what extent your collection is included in normal household insurance, or whether additional insurance might be necessary. You can also make up your own card file with the important data on the cameras (including when and where you bought them, and for what prices!), and leave space for a photo of the camera. As with collecting itself, there is room here for individual preferences. At some shops you may be able to buy prepared file cards at reasonable prices.

How do I Photograph My Collection?

As already mentioned, it is important to take pictures of your collection for good documentation. It is best to photograph the showcase including cameras (with the glass doors open). It may be of interest to the owner personally, if not to the insurance

It is best to store your cameras behind glass to prevent the accumulation of unnecessary dust. Even the best showcase is not entirely dustproof, however, so occasional cleaning is unavoidable.

company, to also show pictures of the best pieces. It is best to set up a professional lighting system, or use a professional flash system. You should work with at least three flashes, set up a light-bowl, and naturally check everything carefully with a light meter. If you don't have all that, you will have to do it more simply. Put a table against a wall and set up a big cardboard sheet (of neutral gray, if possible) so that the camera is on it and the cardboard can be raised in back to attain a shadow-free transition of the background. For lighting, one or two strong halogen lamps (1000 watts each) are suitable. Nitraphoto lamps are also usable, but then if you use day-light film, the color will be affected and must be neutralized with a conversion filter. In any case, in this light you need a good base for your photographing camera. The collection pieces are placed on the cardboard sheet, the lamps placed for the best possible lighting, and the camera set up so that the object appears as fully as possible in the picture. According to availability, you can take pictures with a zoom, close-up, or macro lens, so as to attain as much sharpness as possible. You can also take flash pictures, however doing this with the camera flash right in front is not such a good solution. It is better to use a normal flash attachment with a swinging head above, and a white cardboard some 30 centimeters above the camera for indirect lighting of the collection. You should then be satisfied with the results (if the flash has operated properly). Enlarged to 10 x 15 centimeters, the photos can let your collection be seen, and cut into 6 x 6 squares they can be pasted onto your file cards.

Care and Repair

The leather covering of many cameras will loosen in places with time. Careful gluing with an adhesive will reattach the loose areas.

Naturally, it is nice when cameras come into one's collection in the best possible condition and can be added to the rest immediately. Normal signs of wear should be left on the camera, for it used to be an implement after all. Too much work with paint and brush can only make the camera's appearance worse instead of better.

Still, you should set your own personal standards for the cameras in your collection, as you should always be satisfied with that good piece in the showcase. A Category D piece, in unrepaired and unmaintained condition, will be a constant eyesore until finally replaced with a Category B piece one day. So why not buy it in the desired condition to begin with? That causes less stress and is also cheaper.

In any case, the batteries must be taken out of battery-powered cameras at the start. They can then be packed in small bags, labeled with the name of the camera they belong to, and kept separately, in order to be ready for demonstration purposes or used with the camera. The batteries should not remain in the camera for long, since they leak in time and the acid can erode the interior of the camera.

The camera itself can be dusted with a soft brush, wiped with a damp cloth, or cleaned with spirits (caution — flammable!). Loose leather parts can be attached with an adhesive. The leather itself can be treated with a suitable cleaner or the right color of shoe wax. Thinner, acetone, or similar solutions should not be used on a camera. Whether you use polish on the brass and chrome parts or leave the normal patina is a matter of taste. Wooden cameras should be cleaned only with a damp cloth, and treated with teak oil or furniture polish after drying.

Missing leather parts can be replaced. The problem is usually finding the right leather material. In such cases you can inquire of a shoemaker, upholsterer, hobbyshop owner, or bookbinder. Once you have the material, the pieces must be cut to fit precisely. This should be done as carefully as possible, for even a slight discrepancy will disturb the appearance of the camera afterward. To do so, first take a piece of paper, lay it on the camera, trace the contours with a pencil, and then cut the paper carefully. Chances are, when you now lay the cutout paper on the camera, you will see that it does not fit. Calmly try it with paper a few more times, until it finally fits perfectly! Now apply the paper pattern to the leather, then cut the leather as precisely and carefully as you can. When you have done everything right, moisten the leather (especially the edges!) with glue, let it dry briefly, put the leather on the camera carefully and press it down lightly. It will look like new. Worn spots in paint can be touched up with satin-finish black paint. But experiment first on other objects, so the result on the camera will be perfect and the touched-up spots cannot be recognized.

As for repairing cameras, the general rule is: avoid fast-drying glue and similar products! I once wanted to reattach a loose covering ring to an lens with quick glue. The result was so firm that I could only use the accidentally set 8-by-5-meter shut-ter from then on. It was a real "fixed lens." Before making repairs, you should consider whether you can do such work yourself with good results, or whether it would be better to have a specialist do it, despite the cost. Sticking shutters and other parts can often be made usable for a long period with a breath (no more!) of cleaning gasoline or silicon (don't spray it into the lens!), but usually you have to struggle through the whole lens to find the problem area. If you have limited ability as a fine mechanic, you will often find insoluble problems in reassembly if not before. As for low-priced cameras, it is not worth taking them to the repair shop — in this case it is cheaper to buy a new one. For valuable pieces, you should agree on a price range, for no repair shop can predict the exact repair price in advance. When it costs $90 to repair a defective shutter, you must consider whether it is worth the price or not. Fellow collectors may also be able to recommend good and reasonable repair shops.

Recommended Literature for the Collector

Every collector will want to learn more about his collecting area, the cameras, the firms' histories, and the background information. For this, an extensive array of literature is available.

What you will need first is a catalog, which we have already mentioned elsewhere. In addition, you will need a book of general information on collecting photographica that describes the various areas of collecting — the book you are now reading! Naturally, you will want to delve more deeply into your chosen collecting area and gain specialized knowledge. For that, you can acquire quite an extensive library, only to then find out that one Leica book is better than the other or that one Rollei book puts all the others in the shade. But as a rule, you have already laid out your money by that point and you would have done better to spend it on one or another camera.

In this area as well, we would like to offer you some help. Granted, this is a very subjective choice of books, for they are the ones that I have worked with after getting acquainted with many, though not all:

•Afalter, Udo, *Voigtländer*, Stuttgart 1995.
•Göllner, Peter, *Ernemann-Cameras*, Hückelhofen 1995.
•Heckmann, Hubert E., Minox — *Variations in 8 x 11*, Hückelhofen 1992.
•Hillebrand, R., & Hauschild, H. J., *Nikon Kompendium*, Schaffhausen 1991.
•Kadlubek, Günther, & Hillebrand, Rudolf, *Agfa — Geschichte eines deutschen Weltunternehmens 1867-1997*, Stuttgart 1997.

There is specialist literature on almost every camera system, so that no specialist collector will run out of information. This Agfa history handles not only the historical aspects but also that manufacturer's complete production program.

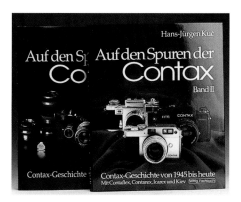

Of the many cameras that Zeiss Ikon has produced, the two books of the Hamburg Contax expert Hans-Jürgen Kuc cover the most interesting areas. Both volumes are published by the Wittig-Verlag of Hückelhofen.

- Hummel, Richard, *Spiegelreflexkameras aus Dresden*, Stuttgart 1995.
- Kemmler, Karl Otto, *Das Kodak-Retina-Kamerabuch*, Stuttgart 1994.
- Kuc, Hans-Jürgen, *Auf den Spuren der Contax*, Kückelhofen 1991.
- Lasney, Denis, *Leica — Das Produkt- und Sammlerbuch*, Augsburg 1995
- Lea, Rudolph, *Register of 35 mm SLR-Cameras*, Hückelhofen 1993.
- Prochnow, Claus, *Rollei-Report 1, Rollei-Report 2, Rollei-Report 3*, Stuggart 1993.
- Shell, Bob, & Richter, Günther, *Canon-Handbuch*, Munich 1994.

These examples represent the present situation, especially in terms of price guides and availability. I know of four more books not listed here that I would like to have in my library. Unfortunately, these books are no longer available. To date I have looked in vain at photo meets and antique shops. The Kodak book by Brian Coe was still selling for $50 a year ago and now costs only $30. This is an indication that the last copies are being sold and the book will soon be sold out.

Let us now look at the gaps in the literature. Naturally, there are many more new camera books than the few named here — but usually they deal with the same brands of cameras. For example, there is no complete book about Zeiss Ikon. Granted, it would be a tremendous job to list and organize the cameras of the many mergers that produced ICA and later Zeiss Ikon, some of which have appeared under three different trade names as well as with varied equipment. There are no Zeiss-Ikon books at hand that could support such a lot of data by citing reliable dates. Many German manufacturers whose cameras hold prominent places in collections today are also missing. The long-awaited Agfa book recently appeared under the title *Agfa — Geschichte eines deutschen Weltunternehmens von 1867-1997*.

You can obtain photo books from photo dealers and bookstores. If problems in obtaining them arise, probably the most inclusive selection of photo books in Germany is to be found at Lindemanns, Nadlerstrasse 10, 70173 Stuttgart.

Collectors' Journals and Clubs

Various publications can keep you informed regarding the current collectors' market, addresses, photo show dates, various collecting areas, and cameras. The best-known photo magazines can be had at any kiosk. The real collectors' journals, which go considerably more deeply and thoroughly into the material, can be obtained only from a few photo dealers or directly from their publishers. Some of the latter will be listed below. Naturally, the addresses can change as new persons are elected to preside over the clubs. But the current presidents will be able to help in the future as well.

•The "Club Daguerre," c/o Horst Piehl, Parkstrasse 1, 53797 Lohmar, Germany, which publishes its own information sheet and a club journal for its members. The yearly dues are approximately $60.
•The first German Minox Club, c/o H. E. Heckmann, Am Krähenhorst 25, 47269 Duisburg, Germany, publishes its well-done "Minox-Freund" and charges yearly dues of approximately $30.

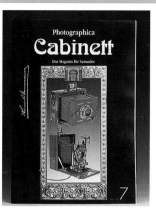

The "Gesellschaft für Photo-Historica" is still relatively new, and its publication *Photographica Cabinett* is edited with much knowledge and involvement.

•The *Photographica Cabinett*, a club magazine of the "Gesellschaft für Photo Historica," c/o Jost Simon, Weidenweg 27, 73733 Esslingen, Germany; its subscription price plus several free advertisements are included in the yearly dues of approximately $30.
•"PHOTO*Deal*" at Kiefernweg 21, 41470 Neuss, Germany, is a collector's magazine without a club affiliation. A year's subscription, for four issues and five lines of free advertising per issue, costs approximately $20.

The one commercially published collectors' magazine, "PHOTO*Deal,*" is involved almost exclusively with classic cameras. In addition, one can find many classified advertisements and a show calendar in this magazine.

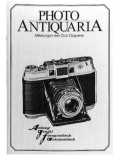

The oldest and very renowned German collectors' group is the "Club Daguerre," which publishes the very competently written journal *Photo Antiquaria*.

The articles in these professionally published periodicals are usually "by collectors for collectors" and thus very informative and interesting. It is sometimes remarkable how much detective ability collectors and authors devote to finding data and details. The classified advertisement section is also important for the collector, as it offers a collectors' market under its "for sale" and "wanted" headings. Other advertisements offer the dates of photo shows, new items on the book market, addresses of camera repair shops, etc.

Many camera manufacturers have their own clubs, whose members have joined for the purpose of exchanging information. Whether Minox, Leica, AGFA, Nikon, Rollei — for almost every manufacturer there is a club, or even more than one, involved with the history and products of that company. Listing all of those clubs at this point is not possibility, for reasons of space as well as because of the constantly changing information. One recommendation for interested parties: write to the editors of

American Nikon authority R. J. Rotoloni is the dedicated editor of the *Nikon Journal*, publication of the "Nikon Historical Society" which he founded. "Bob" Rotoloni is an authority on the early Nikon cameras, about which he has written a well-known book.

"PHOTO*Deal,*" Kiefernweg 21, 41470 Neuss, Germany. They are always up to date and can provide the current address for the club of your choice.

After reading all this, you already know something, but not everything by far, about collecting photographica; you have also acquired suggestions, information, and addresses that will help you go farther. You will find that it is a fascinating hobby as soon as you begin to get closely involved with the subject and acquire the first few collectors' items. In closing, let me state that I hope you will find as much happiness, friendship, and new knowledge as I have.

Günther Kadlubek

There are over 300 members of the "1st German Minox Club", which is devoted completely to the 35 mm and smaller cameras of this renowned brand. Club President Hubert E. Heckmann is known worldwide as probably the greatest expert on Minox cameras.

CATALOG

(B) after a value means that the amount applies only to the box or body without the lens.

WOODEN CAMERAS

Bentzin Travel Camera 13 x 18
1899, wooden plate camera, 13 x 18 cm, Zeiss
Jena Unar 1:5/305 mm, lens panel vertically
and horizontally adjustable. KKK No.
BEZ0400
$200

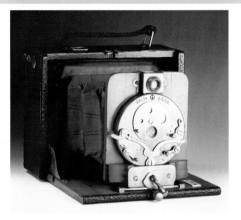

Meyer & Wanner, Strassburg
ca. 1900, wooden camera with black leather,
built for transverse plates, Delta shutter,
central jewel viewfinder over the lens,
standard and interior of the bottom uncovered.
ca. $250

Unknown Wooden Camera
ca. 1910, very decorative transverse wooden
camera, no maker's name, black conical
bellows with red corners, brass lens with
revolver diaphragm. An example of the
perfect handiwork of many unknown camera
carpenters; their work pleases us, but even the
original buyers did not know their names.
ca. $225

Emil Wünsche, Reick-Dresden
1900, travel camera in vertical form, conical
green bellows with reddish-brown corners,
brass lens with revolver diaphragm and "lid-
in-hand" shutter.
$150

Unknown Travel Camera
ca. 1900, wooden travel camera in vertical
form, vertically and horizontally adjustable
lens panel, Hüttig Universal-Aplanat Lloyd
1:8/180 mm, -/100 shutter, black conical
bellows with red corners. Another creation of
an unknown camera carpenter.
ca. $175

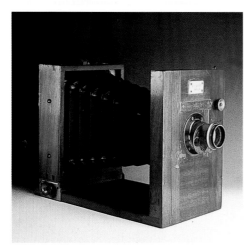

C. P. Goerz Plate Camera
1897, 9 x 12 cm format, brass Rodenstock lens, Bistigmat 9 x 12 cm, horizontally adjustable lens panel, a typical example of an early travel camera.
$200

Russian Studio Camera
1960, the newest Russian studio camera though it doesn't look it, 13 x 18 cm, many possible front and back adjustments.
$225

Friedo Wiesenhaven Travel Camera
1900, special travel camera, brass F 8 lens. The manufacturer is still in existence as a photo company with many branches in Hamburg.
$175

Goldwein 9 x 12 Detective Camera
1890 wooden detective box camera for twelve 9 x 12 cm plates, integrated leather changing bag, periscope lens, simple shutter. KKK No. GOW0010
$450

Contessa-Nettel Tropic Sonnet 10
1922 plate camera, 4.5 x 6 cm, with mahogany or teak case, brown bellows, Tessar 4.5/75 mm, Compur shutter. KKK No. CNT0700
$425

Wünsche Sport 6.5 x 9
1900 wooden camera for 9 x
12 cm plates, brass periscope
lens, simple shutter,
nameplate over lens. KKK
No. WUE0680
$275

Dubroni Equipment
1860 "Photographe de
Poche," wooden camera with
complete chemical equip-
ment for immediate
developing in the camera,
replica by Oberländer. KKK
No. DUB0030
ca. $3000 in original
condition

PLATE CAMERAS

Ihagee Patent Folding Reflex 1110
1924 folding reflex camera, 6.5 x 9
cm with struts, Xenar 4.5/120 mm,
slit shutter -/1000 sec., folding light
shaft. KKK No. IHA0690
$325

Graflex National Graflex Series II
1933 SLR camera, 6 x 7 cm, Tessar 2.8/75 mm, folding lens, large cover cap for light shaft, slit shutter -/1000. KKK No. GRA0390
$140

Goerz Taro Tenax I 9 x 12
1920 plate camera, 9 x 12 cm, Dagor 6.8/150 mm, simple riser, Compur shutter, U standard. KKK No. GOE048
$60

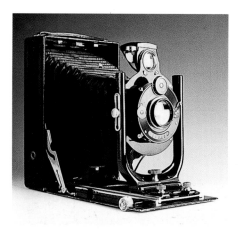

Zeiss-Ikon Maximar 207/9
1927-37 plate camera, 10 x 15 cm, Tessar 4.5/165 mm, Compur -/200. KKK No. ZIK2700
$75

KW Patent Etui 6.5 x 9
1923 plate camera, 6.5 x 9 cm, Meyer Helioplast 1:6/10 cm, Compur -/250, double riser. KKK No. KWE0030
$75

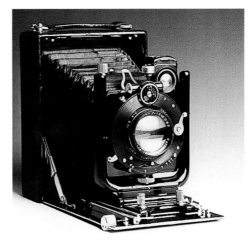

Paul Dette Plate Camera 9 x 12
Year of manufacture unknown, 9 x 12 plate
camera, Laack Polyot 3.9/13.5 cm, Compur.
KKK No. DTT0010
$70

Ica Nelson 225
1915 plate camera, 9 x 12, Tessar 4.5/15 cm,
compound, T. 1-1/150, double riser. KKK No.
ICA0920
$75

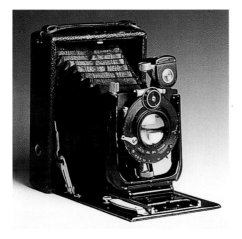

Ica Corrida 157
1910 folding plate camera, 9 x 12 cm, Novar
4.5/135 mm, automatic shutter, adjustable
front standard, KKK No. ICA0200
$50

Huth Plate Camera 13 x 18
1904 wooden travel camera, 13 x 18 cm,
Anastigmat 8/210 mm, simple shutter. KKK
No. HUH0020
$160

Plaubel Makina III
1949-53 roll and flat film camera, 6 x 9 cm,
Anticomar adjustable lens 2.9/100 mm,
Compur -/200, coupled rangefinder, synchronization. KKK No. PLB0120
$285

Zeiss-Ikon Taxo 122/7
1927-31 plate camera, 9 x 12 cm, Novar-
Anastigmat 6.3/135 mm, Derval shutter.
KKK No. ZIK3640
$50

Busch Rathenow Lynx
1908 plate and roll-film camera, 8 x 11 cm,
Aplanat 1:8130 mm, Unicum shutter -/100,
jewel viewfinder, can be adjusted at front.
KKK No. BRW0100
$150

Contessa Nettal Ornito No. 66
1919-26 folding camera, 9 x 12 cm, for plates
and flat film, Citonar 6.3/13.5, Derval -/25 —
/100, double risers. KKK No. CNT0600
$40

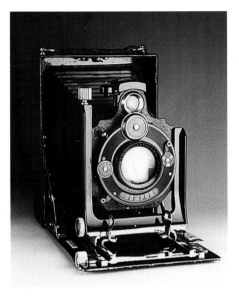

Certo Certotrop 9 x 12
1925 folding camera, 9 x 12 cm, double
Anastigmat Unofokal 4.5/13.5 cm, Compur 1-
/200. KKK No. CER0460
$70

Agfa Standard 208
1928-31 plate camera, 9 x 12 cm, double
Anastigmat 4.5/13.5 cm, Agfa shutter -/200,
jewel and frame viewfinder. KKK No.
AGF3340
$75

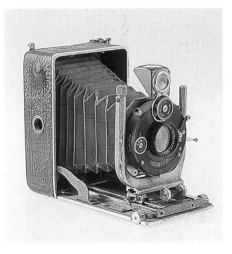

Goerz Tenax 9 x 12
1915-20 plate camera, 9 x 12 cm, Syntor 6.8/
130 mm, Compur -/250, double riser. KKK
No. GOE0611
$60

Voigtländer Bergheim 4.5 x 6 Luxus
1923-27 plate camera, 4.5 x 6 cm, Heliar 4.5/
75 mm, Compur -/200, brown leather, gilded
fittings. KKK No. VOL0260
$900

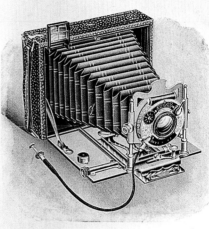

Brieftaschen-Kamera „Patrizia".

Ernemann Heag II Series I
1911-25 plate camera, 10 x 15 cm, Tessar 4.5/
16.5 cm, adjustable front standard, Bob
shutter. KKK No. ERN1280
$40

Spitzer Patrizia
1910 folding plate camera, 9 x 12 cm, Dagor
6.8/135 mm, Espi or Koilos shutter -/300,
adjustable front. KKK No. SPZ0800
$100

Spitzer Atlantica
1910 folding plate camera, 9 x 12 cm, Polynar
6.8/140 mm, Espi shutter -/300 mm, red
bellows, adjustable front. KKK No. SPZ0100
$85

Zeiss-Ikon Volta 146/1
1927/31 plate camera, 9 x 12 cm, Novar-
Anastigmat 8.8/13.5 cm, Derval -/100, jewel
viewfinder. KKK No. ZIK 3896
$40

ROLL-FILM CAMERAS

Balda Baldi 29
1950 KB folding camera with
integrated viewfinder, Color-
Baldanar 2.9/80 mm, Pronto shutter -
/200. KKK No. BAL0840
$50

Ernst Gezi II
1952 roll-film camera 4 x 4, Achromat 11/60 mm, simple shutter, straight-through and reflex viewfinder. KKK No. EST0030
$75

Houghton Ensign E 29
1924-32 wooden box with blue leather, 6 x 9, Meniskus lens, simple shutter. KKK No. HOU0140
$40

Foth Fothflex I
1924-36 twin lens reflex camera, 6 x 6, Anastigmat 3.5/75 mm, slit shutter -/500, distance setting at front above lever. KKK No. FOT0090
$125

Agfa Automatic 66
1956 folding roll-film camera, 6 x 6 cm, Color-Solinar 3.5/75 mm, selenium light meter with pneumatic automatic lighting. KKK No. AGF0760
$700

Agfa Synchro-Box (Box 600)
1949-58 box camera, 6 x 9 cm for roll film,
Meniskus lens 11/105 mm, simple shutter, Art
Deco front. KKK No. AGF 1250.
$20

Dr. Mozar Diana Box
1950 Bakelite box, 6 x 9, Meniskus 1:11,
simple shutter. KKK No. MOZ0010
$65

Dacora Daci
1948 metal box, 6 x 6 for roll film, Meniskus
1:9, simple shutter, rounded corners. KKK
No. DAC0010
$25

Dacora Digna 6 x 6 Pronto
1954 roll-film camera, 6 x 6 cm, with
extending lens, Correlar 2.9/8 cm, Pronto -/
200. KKK No. DAC0410
$50

Cima Luxette S
1954 roll-film camera, 4 x 4 cm, with
Roeschlein Dymat 7.7/50 mm, Synchro-
Cylux 1/25 and 1/100 sec. KKK No.
CIM0060
$35

Contessa-Nettel Piccolette 201
1921-26 folding roll-film camera with Tessar
4.5, Compur shutter. KKK No. CNT0620
$50

Coronet 4-4 Mark II
Year unknown, Bakelite roll-film camera, 4 x
4, gray-black case, Meniskus lens, simple
shutter. KKK No. COT0160
$15

Coronet Ambassador
1955, roll-film box, 6 x 9, Meniskus lens,
simple shutter, extending panels ahead of
jewel viewfinder. KKK No. COT0020
$20

Bilora Bella 66 Neu '6
1962-63 roll-film camera, 6 x 9, Biluskop 8/
70 mm, simple shutter, smooth upper part.
KKK No. BIL0160
$25

Bilora Bellaluxa 4 x 4
196-63 roll-film camera, 4 x 4 cm, Biluskop
1:8, simple shutter, built-in flash, fast shift
lever. KKK No. BIL0190
$25

Bilora Bellina 127
1962 roll-film camera, 4 x 4 cm, Biloxar
1:5.6, 1/30-1/125 shutter, silvered front, fast
winding. KKK No. BIL0210
$30

Tiranti Summa Report
1954 plate and roll-film camera, 6 x 9, Xenar
4.5/105 and Xenar 6.8/65 mm, Synchro-
Compur -/500, rare, only 100 were made.
KKK No. TIR0010
$3000

Welta Perfekta
1934 twin lens roll-film camera, 6 x 6,
Trioplan 3.5/7.5 cm, Compur -/300. KKK No.
WEL0270
$160

Rolleiflex 2.8 F
1960 twin lens reflex camera with Planar 2.8/
80 mm, Synchro-Compur -/500, selenium
light meter, top line model of the classic TLR.
KKK No. ROL1080
$600

Kodak Brownie Cresta II
1956-59 Bakelite roll-film
camera, 6 x 6 cm, Kodet
lens, simple shutter. KKK
No. KOD0780
$15

Kochmann/Wefo Meister-Korelle
1950-52 roll-film SLR, 6 x 6 cm, Primotar
3.5/85 mm, adjustable lens, light shaft. KKK
No. KOC0170
$900

Bentzin Primarette
1929-37 folding twin lens roll-film camera, 4
x 6.5 cm, Tessar 3.5/75 mm, Compur -/300,
separate bellows for viewfinder and photo
lens. KKK No. BEZ0210
$875

Zeiss-Ikon Ikoflex III 853/16
1939-40 twin lens reflex camera, 6 x 6 cm
for roll film, Tessar 2.8/80 mm, Compur-
Rapid -/400, carrying case. KKK No.
ZIK2140
$250

Balda Baldix
1953 roll-film camera, 6 x 6 cm, with Baltar
2.9/75 mm, Prontor II, integrated viewfinder.
KKK No. BAL1020
$45

Balda Baldixette
1960 roll-film camera, 6 x 6, with spring tube, Baldar 9/72 mm, simple shutter. KKK No. BAL1040
$25

Balda Box
1930 roll-film box, 6 x 9, Meniskus, simple shutter. KKK No. BAL0120
$35

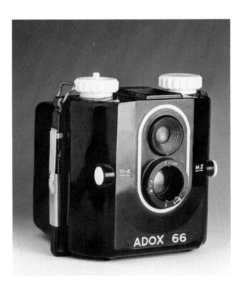

Balda Super Pontura
1936-39 roll-film camera, 4.5 x 6 and 6 x 9 cm, Trioplan 4.5/105 mm, rangefinder, Compur-Rapid -/400. KKK No. BAL1480
$225

Adox 66
1950-58 Bakelite box, 6 x 6 cm for roll film, Meniskus 1:8, simple shutter. KKK No. ADO0030
$30

Beier Beirax
1938 roll-film camera, 6 x 9 cm, Meritar 4.5/105 mm, Tempor -/250, postwar version with integrated viewfinder. KKK No. BEI0120
$50

APM Rajar No. 6
1929 roll-film camera, 6 x 9 cm, made of Bakelite, Meniskus, simple shutter. KKK No. APM0100
$40

Ising Pucky
1949 twin lens roll-film box, 6 x 6, made of Bakelite, Achromat 7.7/8 cm, big central jewel viewfinder, simple shutter. KKK No. ISI0040
$25

Ising Puck
1948 roll-film camera, 3 x 4 cm, extending lens, Trinar 3.5/4.5 cm, Prontor II -/250. KKK No. ISI0040
$75

Belca Belfoca
1953 roll-film folding camera, 6 x 9 cm,
bonar 6.3/105 mm, Binor -/100, folding
viewfinder. KKK No. BEL0030
$40

Agfa-Ansco Shur Flash
1940 roll-film box, 6 x 9, Meniskus, simple
shutter, telescopic viewfinder. KKK No.
ANS0900
$15

Beier Precisa II
1952 roll-film folding camera, 6 x 6 cm,
Meritar 3.5/75 mm, Tempor -/250, case
release. KKK No. BEI0500
$40

Ernemann Ernette
1926 flat-film folding camera, 4.5 x 6 cm for
film packs, Achromat, simple shutter, frame
viewfinder. KKK No. ERN0780
$175

Dr. Rodehüser Panta I
1950 roll-film camera, 4 x 6.5 cm with spring tube, Steinar 2.9/75 mm, Prontor SVS -/300. KKK No. ROD0010
$100

Ernemann Rolf I
1922-25 folding roll-film camera, 4.5 x 6 cm for roll film, Anastigmat 1:7.5, simple shutter. KKK No. ERN2760
$50

Franka Solido Record T
1960 roll-film camera, 6 x 6/4 x 4 cm, lens 1:8/70 mm, simple shutter, gray leather. KKK No. FRK540
$45

Genos Rapid
1950 roll-film box, 6 x 6 cm, made of Bakelite, Meniskus, simple shutter, big central jewel viewfinder. KKK No. GEN0050
$25

Indra Camera GmbH Indra Lux
1949 streamlined 4 x 4 roll-film camera made
of Bakelite, Rau Achromat 7.7/60 mm, simple
shutter, rare. KKK No. IND0010
$140

Ansco Cadet B-2
1947 roll-film box, 6 x 9 cm, Meniskus,
simple shutter, jewel viewfinder. KKK No.
ANS0370
$10

Agfa-Ansco Shur Shot Regula
1932 roll-film box, 6 x 9, Meniskus, simple
shutter, cream-colored recessed front
decoration. KKK No. ANS0910
$30

Agfa Box 50
1949 roll-film box, 6 x 9, Meniskus, simple
shutter, built-in yellow filter. KKK No.
AGF1191
$20

Agfa Billy I
1952 roll-film folding camera, 6 x 9, Agnar
6.3/105 mm, Pronto -/200, see-through
viewfinder. KKK No. AGF0816
$50

Agfa Billy Record I
1950 roll-film folding camera, 6 x 9 cm,
Radionar 4.5/105 mm, Pronto -/200, see-
through viewfinder, case release. KKK No.
AGF1081
$60

Agfa Record III
1954 roll-film folding camera, 6 x 9 cm,
Solinar 4.5/105 mm, Synchro-Compur, -/500,
uncoupled rangefinder. KKK No. AGF2560
$140

Agfa Isolette I
1952 roll-film folding camera, 6 x 6, Agnar
4.5/85 cm, Pronto -/200. KKK No. AGF1681
$40

Agfa Isolette III
1951-58 roll-film folding camera, 6 x 6 cm, Solinar, 3.5/75 mm, Synchro-Compur -/500, uncoupled rangefinder. KKK No. AGF1734
$110

Agfa Billy O
1937 roll-film folding camera, 4 x 6.5 cm, Solinar 3.9/75 mm, Compur -/300 mm, folding and jewel viewfinder. KKK No. AGF0880
$95

Agfa Isolette L
1957-60 roll-film folding camera for KB 24 x 36 mm and 6 x 6 cm, Color-Apotar 4.5/85 mm, Pronto -/200, selenium light meter. KKK No. AGF1760
$90

Agfa Isorette
1937-42 roll-film folding camera, 6 x 6 cm, with black upper part, Apotar 4.5/8.5 cm, Compur /300 (later sold as Isolette), rare. KKK No. AGF1640
$75

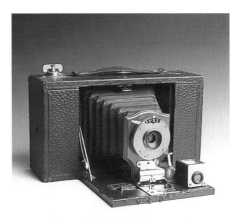

Agfa-Box 14 (Trolix-Box)
1936-41 roll-film box, 6 x 9 cm, made of
Bakelite, periscope 11/100 mm, simple
shutter. KKK No. AGF1260
$65

Kodak No. 3 Folding Brownie
1905-15 roll-film camera, 3.25 x 4.25 inch,
Meniskus lens, Kodak Automatic shutter.
KKK No. KOD0890
$40

Braun Paxina IIb
1952-57 roll-film spring-tube camera, 6 x 6,
with Praxar 8.0/75 mm, simple shutter. KKK
No. BRA1270
$40

Voigtländer Bessa 4.5 x 6/6 x 9
1938 roll-film folding camera with two
formats, rangefinder, Helomar 3.5/105 mm,
Compur-Rapid -/400. KKK No. VOL0370
$95

Adox Trumpf
1934-45 roll-film folding camera, 4.5 x 6/6 x
9 cm, Adoxar 4.5/105 mm, Vario shutter -/
100, KKK No. ADO0470
$40

Rietzschel Roll-Tip
1923 roll-film folding camera, 6 x 9 cm, Tri-
Linear Anastigmat 7.5/105 mm, Pronto
shutter, -/100. KKK No. RIE394
$40

Meopta Flexaret Automat
1962-63 twin lens roll-film camera, 6 x 6 cm,
Belar 3.5/80 mm, Prestor shutter, -/500. KKK
No. MEO0160
$70

Agfa Box 44 "Preisbox"
1932 box camera, 6 x 9 cm, with metal case,
Meniskus 1:11, simple camera, also called "4
Mark Box." KKK No. AGF1170
$45

Agfa Box 64 ("Spezial" Box)
1931 box camera, 6 x 9, with metal case,
Meniskus 11/105 mm, with three-point
distance setting, simple shutter. KKK No.
AGF1211
$45

Reporter Max II (Kaufhof)
1954 Max II (Bilora Belle 4 x 6.5) roll-film
camera, 4 x 6.5, for 127 film, simple shutter,
equipment carrier. KKK No. REP0067
$35

GOMZ Lubitel-2
1970 twin lens Reflex camera made of
Bakelite, Lomo lens, 4.5 x 7.5 mm, central
shutter -/250, automatic release, flash
synchronization. KKK No. GMZ0180
$40

Bilora Boy
1950-52 roll-film box, 4 x 6.5 cm, made of
Bakelite, 127 roll film, Meniskus 1:11, simple
shutter, also made of wine-red Bakelite. KKK
No. BIL0310
$20

Vredeborch Adina
1950 roll-film box, 6 x 9 cm, with metal case,
Meniskus, simple shutter, Art Deco front.
KKK No. VRE0010
$35

Rolleiflex 4 x 4
1957-63 twin lens reflex camera, 4 x 4 cm, for
127 film, Xenar 3.5/60 mm, Compur MXV -/
500. KKK No. ROL1250
$200

Ernemann Bobette I
1925 roll-film folding camera, 18 x 24 mm,
Ernoplast 4.5/5 cm, frame viewfinder,
Ernemann shutter, -/100. KKK No. ERN0530
$500

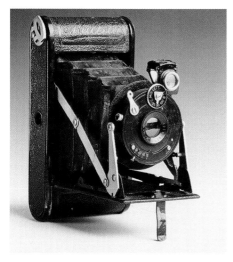

Mullett
Year unknown, folding roll-film camera for
127 film, Spezial-Aplanat 11/85, V: Mullett
25-100, jewel and flap viewfinder. KKK No.
MUL0010
$60

Altissa Eho Box 6 x 9
1932-39 roll-film box, 6 x 9 cm, with metal
case, Duplar 1:11, simple shutter. KKK No.
ALT0380
$35

Houghton Ensign Ful-Vue Super
1938-45 twin lens box camera with light
shaft, Meniskus lens, simple shutter, metal
case with hammered finish. KKK No.
HOU0280
$25

Metropolitan Ind., Clix-O-Flex
1969 tall Bakelite box for 127 roll-film, with
3 x 4 cm format, Maestar Lens F. 57.5 mm,
chromed light shaft. KKK No. MEI0050
$20

Goerz Tengor Rollfilm 6 x 9
1920-25 folding roll-film camera, Frontar 9/
11 cm, Goerz 25-100, adjustable front. KKK
No. GOE0540
$35

Kodak No. 2A Folding Autographic Brownie
1915-26 folding roll-film camera, 2.25 x 4.25
inches, for 116 film, Achromat 1:7.9, Kodak -
/50 shutter. KKK No. KOD0920
$15

Kochmann Korelle 4.5 x 6
1931 folding folding camera, 3 x 4, for 127
film, Ludwig Enoldar 2.9/5 cm, Compur -/
500, folding viewfinder. KKK No. KOC0120
$100

Tiranty Coronet
1950 roll-film folding camera, 6 x 9, Boyer
Topaz 6.3/100 mm, -/125 sec. shutter, jewel
viewfinder. KKK No. TIY0030
$75

Nagel Ranca
1930-31 roll-film camera, 3 x 4 cm, for 127
film, Anastigmat 4.5/5 cm, Pronto -/100,
folding viewfinder. KKK No. NAG0240
$120

Voigtländer Brillant
1934 twin lens reflex camera, 6 x 6 cm, made of Bakelite, Voigtar 6.3/7.5 cm, Compur -/ 300, "Landschaft-Gruppe-Portrait" (land-scape-group-portrait) distance setting. KKK No. VOL0660
$50

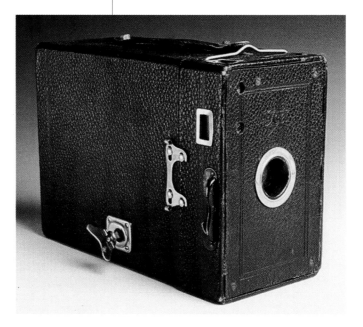

Ica Orix Box 3
1924 box camera, 6.5 x 11 cm, wooden case with leather, Meniskus with close-up lens, simple shutter. KKK No. ICA0990
$130

Voigtländer Brillant
1933 twin lens reflex camera, 6 x 6 cm, made
of Bakelite, Skopar 4.5/7.5 cm, Compur -/
300, folding light shaft. KKK No. VOL0650
$60

Balda Juwella II
1938 roll-film folding camera with three
formats: 4.5 x 6, 6 x 6, 6 x 9 cm, Anastigmat
4.5/10.5, Balda shutter, -/25/100. KKK No.
BAL1240
$60

Herlango Renox, RF 6 x 9
ca. 1930 roll-film folding camera, Juwella-
Anast. 6.3/10.5, shutter -/25-/100, frame
viewfinder. KKK No. HEL0040
$50

Lumiere Box Nr. 49
1938 box camera, 8 x 10.5 cm for 122 roll
film, metal case, Meniskus, simple shutter.
KKK No. LUM0030
$25

Zeiss-Ikon Ikonette 504/12
1929-31 roll-film folding camera, 4 x 6.5 cm,
Frontar 1:9/80 mm, simple shutter, jewel
viewfinder. KKK No. ZIK2240
$40

MIOM Photax
1937 box camera with two
Bakelite cases and two
formats: 4.5 x 6 and 6 x 9,
Boyer Series VII,
integrated optical
viewfinder. KKK No.
MIV0040
$45

SMALL VIEWFINDER CAMERAS

Agfa Optima 1035 Sensor
1977 small viewfinder camera, 24 x
36 mm, CdS light meter with
electronic shutter (Paratronic), Solitar
S 2.8/40 mm. KKK No. AGF2340
$50

Agfa Parat-I
1963 half-size viewfinder camera, 18 x 24
mm, light regulation via symbol setting,
Color-Apotar 2.8/30 mm. KKK No. AGF2490
$40

Agfa Optima Flash
1977 small viewfinder camera with integrated
folding electronic flash, automatically
programmed shutter, Solinar 2.8/40 mm.
KKK No. AGF2370
$70

Agfa Compact
1980 small viewfinder camera, 24 x 36 mm,
with integrated film advance motor, settable
E-flash, Solinar 2.8/39 mm. KKK No.
AGF1360
$90

Dacora-matic 4D
1960 small viewfinder camera with four
setting keys, light meter, Cassar 2.8/45 mm.
KKK No. DAC0370
$50

Agfa Silette SLE
1958 small viewfinder camera with coupled rangefinder, Color-Solinar 2.8/50 mm. KKK No. AGF2920
$110

Dacora Dignette 125
1960 small viewfinder camera, Isconar 2.8/45 mm, Prontor 125 shutter. KKK No. DAC0600
$25

Agfa Optima Rapid 125 C
1966-72 small viewfinder camera, 24 x 24 mm, for rapid cartridges, automatic flash with selenium cell, Color-Apotar, 2.8/45 mm. KKK No. AGF2430
$25

Arette I D
1957 small viewfinder camera with selenium light meter, coupled rangefinder, Prontor SVS -/300, Xenar 2.8/50 mm. KKK No. AKA0190
$45

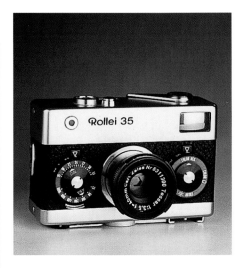

Elop Elca
1949 small viewfinder camera, 24 x 24 mm, simple shutter, Elocar 4.5/3.5 cm. KKK No. ELO0010
$85

Rollei 35
1966-71 small viewfinder camera, 24 x 36 mm, Tessar 3.5/40 mm, Compur shutter, 1/2-1/500 sec., CdS light meter. KKK No. ROL0200
$225

Kodak Retinette II B
1958-59 small viewfinder camera, 24 x 36 mm, selenium light meter, Reomar 2.8/45 mm, Compur-Rapid shutter. KKK No. KOD7230
$60

King Regula Sprinty LK 300
1970-74 small viewfinder camera with selenium light meter, Rectamat shutter, -/300, Color-Isconar 2.8/45 mm. KKK No. KIG1000
$30

Kodak Retina III C
1958-60 small viewfinder camera with
coupled rangefinder and selenium light meter,
adjustable lens, Xenon 2.0/50 mm. KKK No.
KOD6890
$340

Agfa Super Silette
1954 small viewfinder camera with coupled
rangefinder, Synchro-Compur -/500, Solagon
2.0/50 mm. KKK No. AGF2940
$160

AkA Akarette Mod. II
1950 small viewfinder camera with adjustable
lens, tele-wide-angle switch, Xenar 3.5/50
mm, Prontor shutter, -/300. KKK No.
AKA0120
$60

Frankonia Robinette
1950 small viewfinder camera, Cassar 2.9/5
cm, Compur-Rapid shutter, -/500, plastic case
trim with vertical stripe pattern. KKK No.
FRU0010
Rare, no price estimate possible

Finetta 99
1950 small viewfinder camera with adjustable
lens, Finetar 2.8/45 mm, integrated spring
motor, slit shutter, -/1000. KKK No. FIN0120
$125

Camera Corp. of Chicago Perfex 55
1940-47 small viewfinder camera with optical
light meter, rangefinder, Scienar 3.5/5 cm.
KKK No. CCA0050
$50

Canon Canonet G-III 17 QL
1965 small viewfinder camera with coupled
rangefinder, CdS light meter, automatic flash,
Canon lens, 1.7/40 mm. KKK No. CAN1070
$100

Wirgin Edixa I
1954-58 small viewfinder camera with
Ennagon 2,8/45 mm, Pronto -/200. KKK No.
WIR0260
$50

Bolta Photavit IV
1938-50 small viewfinder camera, 24 x 24
mm, in special case, Radionar 3.5/37.5 mm,
Compur-Rapid -/500. KKK No. BOT0080
$100

Braun (Ffm.) Nizo 1000 Elektr.
1969 small viewfinder camera, 24 x 36 mm,
with coupled rangefinder, electrically
controlled shutter, -/1000, flash-cube
attachment. KKK No. NIZ0020
$90

Robot Royal 24
1953 small viewfinder camera, 24 x 24 mm,
with adjustable lens, spring motor, shutter -/
500.
$350

Braun Super-Colorette II B
1957-59 small viewfinder camera with
adjustable lens, selenium light meter, coupled
rangefinder, Culminar 2.8/50 mm. KKK No.
BRA0540
$70

Braun Paxette I M
1953-59 small viewfinder camera with
unconnected rangefinder, quick-shift lever,
Pointar 2.8/45 mm, Prontor SV -/300. KKK
No. BRA0910
$45

Braun Paxette Electromatic II
1961-63 small viewfinder camera with
selenium light meter and automatic flash,
Prontormat-S shutter, Katagon 5.6/40 mm.
KKK No. BRA1090
$40

Bilora Radix 35 BH
1953-55 small viewfinder camera, 24 x 24
mm, Biloxar 3.5/38 mm, shutter -/200. KKK
No. BIL0500
$40

Certo Dollina O
1936-39 small viewfinder camera with
folding lens, Meritar 3.5/5 cm, Junior shutter -
/100. KKK No. CER0540
$45

Agfa Solinette II
1952 small viewfinder camera with folding
lens, Apotar 3.5/50 mm, Prontor-SV shutter -/
300. KKK No. AGF3130
$75

Futura S
1955 small viewfinder camera with adjustable
lens, coupled rangefinder, Synchro-Compur
shutter -/500, Evar 2.0/50 mm. KKK No.
FUR0030
$200

FED-2 (red)
1955-70 small viewfinder camera with slit
shutter -/500, coupled rangefinder, Industar
26 M 2.8/5 cm, red leather. KKK No.
FED0080
$75

Clarus MS-35
1939 small viewfinder camera, coupled
rangefinder, slit shutter 1/25-1/1000,
Velostigmat 2.8/50 mm. KKK No. CLR0010
$60

Leica Compur (Ring-Compur)
1926-30 small viewfinder camera with Elmar
3.5/50 mm lens, Compur shutter -/300. KKK
No. LEI0120
$6,000

Leica M4
1967-75 small viewfinder camera with
adjustable lens, Summilux 1.4/50, slit shutter
1-1/1000 sec. KKK No. LEI0730
$750 (B)

Argus C3
1940 small viewfinder camera, coupled
rangefinder, angular case, Contar 3.5/50 mm.
KKK No. ARG0190
$60

Ansco Karomat 36
1950-56 small folding camera (made by Agfa,
identical to Karat 36), Xenon 2.0/50 mm,
Compur-Rapid -/500. KKK No. ANS0660
$110

Altissa Altix I

1937-47 small viewfinder camera, rectangular lens plate, Laack Pololyt 3.5/35 mm, shutter 1/25-1/150 sec. KKK No. ALT0120
$40

AKA Arette Automatic S

1959 small viewfinder camera with automatic lighting and selenium light meter, Prontormat, Color-Westanar 2.8/45 mm. KKK No. AKA0260
$50

Voss Diax I b

1956-57 small viewfinder camera with coupled rangefinder, Xenon 2.0/50 mm, fast switching lever, Compur shutter. KKK No. VOS0060
$95

Voigtländer Vito B

1954 small viewfinder camera with Pronto-Prontor SVS shutter, Color-Skopar 3.5/50 mm. KKK No. VOL1860
$40

Zeiss Jena Werra 3
1958-64 small viewfinder camera with
adjustable lens and rangefinder, shutter
tension by turning ring on lens. KKK No.
ZEJ0100
$60

Zeiss-Ikon Contessa LKE
1963-65 small viewfinder camera with
selenium light meter, coupled rangefinder,
Tessar 2.8/50 mm, Prontor 500 LK. KKK No.
ZIK0950
$65

Balda CE 35 (Yangtze-Balda)
1989 small viewfinder camera with folding
lens, Baldanon 2.8/38 mm, electronic shutter
with automatic lighting. KKK No. BAL0360
$125

Beier Beirette SL 400
1977 small viewfinder camera with CdS
automatic lighting, Priomat shutter, Meritar
2.8/45 mm. KKK No. BEI0280
$35

Canon 7
1961-64 small viewfinder camera with
adjustable lens, Canon 0.95/50 mm, slit
shutter 1-1/1000 sec. KKK No. CAN0490
$225

Agfa Iso-Pak
1968 cassette camera, 126 28 x 28 mm,
Parator shutter, Meniskus lens 11/42 mm.
KKK No. AGF1870
$15

Closter IIa (Italian)
1950 small viewfinder camera, Mizar 4.5/50
mm, central shutter -/300. KKK No.
CLO0010
$50

Adox Polomat
1959-64 small viewfinder camera with
coupled selenium light meter, Radionar L 2.8/
45 mm, Pronto LK -/250. KKK No.
ADO0290
$20

Photo Porst Hapo 35
1955 small folding camera with coupled
rangefinder, built by Balda, Prontor SVS -/
300, Enna Haponar 2.8/50 mm. KKK No.
PHP0510
$50

Balda Baldina
1935 small folding camera with optical
viewfinder, case release, Meritar 2.9/50 mm,
Ovus shutter -/200. KKK No. BAL0850
$100

Leidolf Lordomat Standard
1956 small viewfinder camera with adjustable
lens, coupled rangefinder, Lordonar 2.8/50
mm, fast switching lever, Prontor SVS. KKK
No. LDO0120
$60

Zeiss-Ikon Contax I
1931-34 small rangefinder camera with
adjustable lens, slit shutter 1/25-1/1000 sec.,
Tessar 2.8/50 mm. KKK No. ZIK0830
$275 (B)

Agfa Isoly 100 (made by Certex S.A. in
Spain)
Small viewfinder camera with sensor release,
Isitar Special lens. KKK No. AGF1845
$60

Agfa Karat 12
1938 small viewfinder camera for Karat
cartridges, coupled rangefinder, Xenar 2.8/50
mm, Compur-Rapid -/500. KKK No.
AGF1951
$70

Agfa Optima 500 S
1963 small viewfinder camera with light
meter and coupled rangefinder, Color-Solinar
2.8/45 mm, Compur shutter. KKK No.
AGF2300
$90

Agfamatic 300 Sensor
1972 cassette camera, 126 28 x 28 mm,
automatic CdS light meter, sensor release,
Color-Agnar 8.0/44 mm. KKK No. AGF0180
$25

Agfa Karat IV
1954-56 small viewfinder camera, coupled
rangefinder, Solinar 2.8/50 mm, Prontor SVS
-/300. KKK No. AGF2030
$80

Agfa Ambi-Silette de Luxe
1960 luxury version of the Ambi-Silette, case
fitted with snake leather, Color-Solinar 2.8/45
mm, Synchro-Compur -/500. KKK No.
AGF0722
Rare, no price estimate possible

Agfa Super-Solinette
1953 small folding camera with coupled
rangefinder, Solinar 3.5/50 mm, Synchro-
Compur -/500. KKK No. AGF3140
$90

Balda CA 35
1983 small viewfinder camera, Baldanar 2.8/
38 mm, CdS automatic flash. KKK No.
BAL0340
$70

Agfa Le Box Photo
1994 one-way camera, 24 x 36 mm,
Meniskus 1:17, simple shutter. KKK No.
AGF2070
$7.50

Zeiss-Ikon Contax II
1936-43 small viewfinder camera with
adjustable lens, Sonnar 2.0/5 cm, slit shutter
1/1250 sec. KKK No. ZIK0850
$175 (B)

Adox 300
1956-60 small viewfinder camera with
changeable magazine and built-in light meter,
Cassar 2.8/45 mm, Synchro-Compur shutter.
KKK No. ADO0050
$200

Adox Polomat 1
1960-65 small viewfinder camera with
coupled light meter, Radionar L 2.8/45 mm,
Prontor 500 LK. KKK No. ADO0300
$30

Agfa Karat 6.3 Deko
1937 small folding camera with Igestar 6.3/50 mm, deco design on front, Agfa or Vario shutter, comes with carrying loops. KKK No. AGF1920
$45

Altissa Altuca
1951 small viewfinder camera with extending lens tube, Meritar 3.5/75 mm, Junior shutter. KKK No. ALT0300
$40

Braun Paxette II M
1953-58 small viewfinder camera with uncoupled rangefinder, Cassarit 2.8/50 mm, Prontor SVS shutter. KKK No. BRA0960
$65

Canon 2D
1952-55 small viewfinder camera with adjustable lens, Canon 1.8/50 mm, slit shutter 1/25-1/500 sec., about 22,000 made. KKK No. CAN0150
$325

FED-5
1977-80 small viewfinder camera with light meter, adjustable lens, FED 3.5/50 mm, slit shutter. KKK No. FED0220
$40

Finetta 88 black
1954 small viewfinder camera with adjustable lens, Finetar 2.8/45 mm, central shutter, 1/25-1/250 sec., also made with gray leather. KKK No. FIN0110
$65

GOMZ Smena 2
1956 small viewfinder camera with Bakelite case, Triplet-22 4.5/40 mm lens, automatic release, flash synchronization. KKK No. GMZ0340
$20

Kiev 4
1957-79 small viewfinder camera, copy of Contax II, adjustable lens Jupiter-8 2.0/50 mm, slit shutter 1/2-1/1250 sec. KKK No. KIV0070
$80

AKA Arette A
1957 small viewfinder camera, Arettar 2.8/45 mm, Vario/Prontor SVS shutter. KKK No. AKA0210
$40

Altissa Altix III
1959 small viewfinder camera with adjustable lens, Meritar 2.9/50 mm, Vebur shutter -/250. KKK No. ALT0170
$60

Kodak Instamatic 500
1963-66 high-priced small viewfinder camera, 28 x 28 mm for 126 cassette film, selenium light meter, Xenar 2.8/38 mm, Compur -/500. KKK No. KOD4150
$90

King Regula IIId
1956-58 small viewfinder camera with adjustable lens, Westanar 2.8/45 mm, built-in light and rangefinders, Prontor-SVS. KKK No. KIG0370
$50

Leitz Leica Standard (E) black
1932-48 small camera with adjustable lens,
Elmar 3.5/50 mm, telescopic viewfinder on
top, slit shutter 1/20-1/500 sec. KKK No.
LEI0200
$375 (B)

Leitz Leica II (D) black
1932-48 small camera with adjustable lens,
Elmar 3.5/50 mm, rangefinder, slit shutter 1/
20-1/500 sec. KKK No. LEI0150
$325

Kodak Retinette Type 012 F
1949-51 small folding camera, Kodak
Angenieux 4.5/50 mm, Atos shutter -/250,
complete with Pathe lens and shutter in
France. KKK No. KOD7050
$90

Fuji Fujica 35-SE
1967 small camera with selenium light meter,
coupled rangefinder, Fujinon 2.8/4.5 cm, Fuji
Synchro MXL, B, 1-1000 sec. KKK No.
FUJ0895
$35

Robot II
1934-50 small camera with spring motor, optical viewfinder on top, Tessar 2.8/3 cm, rotating shutter -/250 sec.
$300 (B)

FAP Norca
1938 small viewfinder camera with Bakelite case, Berthiot Flor 3.5/50 mm in extending tube, central shutter -/175. KKK No. FAP0080
$100

Bencini Comet S
1950 roll-film camera, 3 x 4 cm for 127 film, Achromat 1:11, simple shutter -/50, flash synchronization. KKK No. BEC0040
$25

Wirgin Edinex BM
Small viewfinder camera with optical light
meter, Prontor-SV-300, Cassar 2.8/50 mm,
integrated viewfinder. KKK No. WIR0151
$120

Witt Iloca Automatic
1959 small camera with selenium light meter,
coupled rangefinder, Compur-Rapid, Cassarit
2.8/50 mm. KKK No. WIT0070
$55

Balda 104
1965 cassette camera, 28 x 28 mm for 126
film, Isco Meniskus lens, simple shutter,
imitation selenium light meter on front.
KKK No. BAL0130
$15

Zeiss-Ikon Contessamat
1964-65 small camera with automatic light
regulation, coupled light meter,
Prontormatic shutter -/125, Color-Pantar
2.8/45. KKK No. ZIK1030
$65

SMALL REFLEX CAMERAS

Agfa Ambiflex II
1959-63 SLR camera with adjustable
lens, Solinar 2.8/50 mm, selenium
light meter, changeable viewfinder.
KKK No. AGF0740
$125 (B)

Agfa Selectaflex I
1963 small SLR camera with adjustable lens,
Solinar 2.8/50 mm, Prontor-Reflex, selenium
light meter. KKK No. AGF2690
$175 (B)

Agfa Optima Reflex
1960 small twin lens reflex camera, selenium
light meter, automatic light measurement,
Color-Apotar 2.8/45 mm. KKK No. AGF2470
$160

Braun Paxette Reflex Autom.
1959-62 small SLR camera with adjustable
lens, Cassarit 2.8/50 mm, selenium light
meter, Synchro-Compur -/500. KKK No.
BRA1370
$90 (B)

Kuribayashi Petriflex 7
1964 small SLR camera with adjustable lens,
Petri 1.8/55 mm, slit shutter -/1000, selenium
light meter. KKK No. KUR0410
$200 (B)

Tokyo Kogaku Topcon RE Super
1963 small SLR camera with CdS automatic
lighting (TTL), Topcor 1.4/5.8 cm adjustable
lens, slit shutter -/1000 sec., changeable
viewfinder system. KKK No. TKK0390
$75 (B)

Nikon Nikkormat FT3
1977 small SLR camera with adjustable lens,
TTL opening measuring, slit shutter -/1000
sec. KKK No. NIN0150
$200 (B)

Pignons Alpa Reflex
1942 small SLR camera with light shaft,
Alpar 2.9/50 mm, slit shutter -/1000 sec.
KKK No. PIG0030
$500

Pignons Alpa 9d
1965-69 small SLR camera with CdS TTL
measurement, adjustable lens Makro-Switar
1.8/50 mm, slit shutter -/1000 sec. KKK No.
PIG0190
$800

Olympus Pen F

1963-66 small SLR camera for half-format 18 x 24 mm, TTL light meter, Zuiko adjustable lens 1.4/40 mm, slit shutter -/500. KKK No. OLY1160
$150 (B)

Zeiss-Ikon Contarex I

1959-66 small SLR camera with Planar adjustable lens 2.0/50 mm, selenium light meter, slit shutter -/1000 sec. KKK No. ZIK0740
$400 (B)

Bauer-Bosch RX 1

1978 small SLR camera with Neovaron adjustable lens 1.7/50 mm (K-Bajonett), TTL light meter, slit shutter -/1000 sec. KKK No. BAU0020
$300 (B)

Agfa Selectronic 2

1980 small SLR camera with Agfa-Color adjustable lens 1.9/50 mm (K-Bajonett), TTL light meter with automatic timing, slit shutter. KKK No. AGF2630
$110 (B)

Rolleiflex SL 26
1968-71 small SLR camera for 126 cassette
film, Tessar adjustable lens 2.8/40 mm,
Compur shutter -/500. KKK No. ROL1280
$115 (B)

Ihagee Exakta Real
1967 small SLR camera with Travenar
adjustable lens 2.8/50 mm, TTL light meter,
slit shutter 2-1/1000 sec., two case releases.
KKK No. IHA2470
$1500 (B)

Ihagee Exakta Varex IIa
1958-60 small SLR camera with slit shutter
12-1/1000 sec., Travenar 2.8/50 mm,
adjustable viewfinder. KKK No. IHA2380
$90 (B)

Ihagee Kine-Exacta (angled loop)
1937 small SLR camera with Tessar adjustable lens 2.8/5 cm, slit shutter 12-1/1000 sec.
KKK No. IHA0460
$750 (B)

Ihagee Exa 500
1966-69 small SLR camera with Tessar adjustable lens 2.8/50 mm, slit shutter 1/2-1/500 sec. KKK No. IHA2240
$45 (B)

Ihagee Elbaflex VX 1000
1969-70 small SLR camera with Tessar adjustable lens 2.8/50 mm, adjustable viewfinder, slit shutter 12-1/1000 sec. KKK No. IHA2010
$90

Ihagee Exa 1b
1983-84 small SLR camera with Tessar adjustable lens 2.8/50 mm, flap shutter 1/30-1/175 sec. KKK No. IHA2180
$70 (B)

Ihagee RTL 1000
1969-70 small SLR camera with Pancolar adjustable lens 1.8/50 mm, adjustable viewfinder, slit shutter 8-1/1000 sec. KKK No. IHA2480
$70 (B)

Nikon F Photomic
1962 small SLR camera with Nikkor
adjustable lens 1.4/5.8 cm, slit shutter 1-1/
1000 sec., adjustable viewfinder with
selenium rangefinder. KKK No. MIR0340
$400 (B)

Miranda Sensorex
1968-72 small SLR camera with Miranda
adjustable lens 1.8/50 mm, adjustable
viewfinder, TTL light meter, slit shutter -/
1000 sec. KKK No. MIR0340
$65 (B)

Miranda S
1959 small SLR camera with Miranda
adjustable lens 2.8/5 cm, adjustable
viewfinder, slit shutter 1/30-1/500 sec. KKK
No. MIR0060
$110 (B)

Kilfitt Mecaflex
1960 small SLR camera, 24 x 24 mm, with
Kilar adjustable lens 3.5/40 mm, light shaft,
all controls under case lid, Prontor-Reflex -/
300. KKK No. KIF0010
$750

Rectaflex 1000
1948 small SLR camera with Angenieux
adjustable lens 2.5/50 mm, slit shutter -/1000
sec. KKK No. REF0040
$300 (B)

Voigtländer Bessamatic
1958-63 small SLR camera with Color-
Skopar adjustable lens 2.8/50 mm, selenium
light meter, Synchro-Compur -/500. KKK No.
VOL0520
$90 (B)

Wirgin Edixa-Mat Reflex C-L
1963 small SLR camera with Cassaron
adjustable lens 2.8/50 mm, selenium light
meter, adjustable viewfinder, slit shutter 1-1/
1000 sec. KKK No. WIR0800
$80

Wirgin Edixa Electronica
1961-65 small SLR camera with Culminar
adjustable lens 2.8/50 mm, fully automatic
light adjustment via selenium light meter.
KKK No. WIR560
$165 (B)

Revueflex LTL (made by Wirgin)
1968 small SLR camera with Iscovitar
adjustable lens 2.8/50 mm, slit shutter 1-1/
1000 sec., TTL light meter (identical to Edixa
Prismat LTL). KKK No. REV0720
$75 (B)

Rolleiflex SL 350
1974-76 small SLR camera with Planar
adjustable lens 1.4/50 mm, TTL light meter,
slit shutter 1-1/1000 sec. KKK No. ROL1380
$280 (B)

KW Practica Nova B
1965-67 small SLR camera with Tessar
adjustable lens 2.8/50 mm, selenium light
meter, slit shutter 1/2-1/500 sec. KKK No.
KWE1790
$60 (B)

KW Praktiflex II M40
1947-49 small SLR camera with Tessar
adjustable lens 3.5/5 cm (M40 threading), slit
shutter 1/25-1/500 sec., light shaft. KKK No.
KWE2020
$100 (B)

Minolta SR-T 101
1966 small SLR camera with MC-Rokkor-PG adjustable lens 1.2/58 mm, TTL opening control, slit shutter 1-/1000 sec. KKK No. MIN2370
$75 (B)

Uca Ucaflex
1951 small SLR camera with Ucalux adjustable lens 1.8/5 cm, reflex and see-through viewfinder, slit shutter -/1000 sec. KKK No. UCA0020
$500

KW Pentacon Super
1968-72 small SLR camera with Pancolor adjustable lens 1.4/55 mm, adjustable viewfinder, TTL light meter, motor connection, slit shutter 1-1/2000 sec. KKK No. KWE1060
$275 (B)

KW Praktica I
1949-50 small SLR camera with Tessar adjustable lens 3.5/5 cm, slit shutter 1/2-1/500 sec., light shaft, flash not synchronized. KKK No. KWE1150
$90 (B)

KW Practica IV B
1961-64 small SLR camera with Tessar adjustable lens 2.8/50 mm, selenium light meter, slit shutter -/500. KKK No. KWE1210
$60 (B)

Kiev 15 TEE
1974-80 small SLR camera with Helios-81 adjustable lens 2.0/50 mm, TTL automatic light meter, slit shutter 1/2-1/1000 sec. KKK No. KIV0160
$110 (B)

Kiev 10 Automat
1965-74 small SLR camera with Helios-81 adjustable lens 2.0/50 mm, selenium light meter with automatic flash, slit shutter 1/2-1/1000 sec. KKK No. KIV0150
$125 (B)

Krasnogorsk Zenit C
1955-61 small SLR camera with Industar-50 adjustable lens 3.5/5 cm, slit shutter -/500 sec. KKK No. KRA0500
$75 (B)

Krasnogorsk Zenit E
1965-80 small SLR camera with Helios-44 adjustable lens 2.0/58 mm, selenium light meter, slit shutter -/500 sec. KKK No. KRA0520
$40 (B)

King Regula Reflex 2000 CTL
1969-75 small SLR camera with Westromat adjustable lens 1.9/50 mm, TTL light meter, slit shutter 1-1/2000 sec. KKK No. KIG0820
$230 (B)

Kodak Retina Reflex
1956-58 small SLR camera with Xenon adjustable lens 2.0/50 mm, selenium light meter, Synchro-Compur -/500. KKK No. KOD6980
$100

Konica Autoreflex T
1970 small SLR camera with Hexanon adjustable lens 1.8/52 mm, TTL light meter, slit shutter, 1-1/1000 sec. KKK No. KON0130
$140 (B)

Canon Pellix QL
1966-70 small SLR camera with Canon FL
adjustable lens 1.8/50 mm, slit shutter,
semitransparent mirror, slit shutter -/1000 sec.
KKK No. CAN1520
$140 (B)

Canon F-1
1971-76 small SLR camera with FD adjustable lens 1.4/50 mm, TTL opening control,
adjustable viewfinder, motor connection,
many accessories. KKK No. CAN0840
$210 (B)

Fujica ST-701
1971 small SLR camera with Fujinon
adjustable lens 1.8/55 mm, TTL light meter,
slit shutter 1-1/1000. KKK No. FUJ1570
$90 (B)

Asahin Pentax ME-F
1982-85, first small SLR camera with
autofocus through use of special zoom 2.8/35-
70 AF, TTL light meter, slit shutter 4-1/2000,
KKK No. ASA0480
$125 (B)

Leitz Leicaflex SL
1974-76 small SLR camera with selective
TTL opening control, slit shutter 1-1/2000
sec, spare battery compartment. KKK No.
LEI1041
$850 (B)

Zeiss-Ikon Contaflex 126
1970-73 small SLR camera for 126 cassette
film, automatic flash, slit shutter -/500, Tessar
2.8/45 mm. KKK No. ZIK0720
$140

Zeiss-Ikon Contaflex Super
1959-63 small SLR camera with adjustable
front lens for lens sets, Tessar 2.8/50 mm,
Synchrom-Compur -/500, selenium light
meter. KKK No. ZIK06010
$125

GOMZ Sport
1935 small SLR camera, along with the Kine-
Exacta one of the first small SLR cameras,
Industar 10 adjustable lens 3.5/50 mm, slit
shutter -/500. KKK No. GMZ0520
$275

Agfa Colorflex I
1958-63 small SLR camera with replaceable viewfinder (prism and light shaft), Color-Apotar 2.8/50 mm, Prontor-Reflex shutter -/300. KKK No. AGF1340
$100

Canonflex RM
1961-64 small SLR-camera with selenium light meter, slit shutter 1-1/2000 sec., Canonmatic adjustable lens 1.8/50 mm. KKK No. CAN0610
$85

Tokyo Kog. Beseler/Topcon B
1959-61 small SLR camera with replaceable viewfinder, Auto Topcor adjustable lens 1.8/5.5 cm, slit shutter -/1000 sec. KKK No. TKK0230
$60 (B)

Kodak Instamatic Reflex
1968-70 SLR camera for 126 cassette film, CdS light meter with automatic lighting, Xenar adjustable lens 2.8/45 mm. KKK No. KOD4310
$90 (B)

KW Praktica LLC
1969-75 first small SLR camera with motorized film advance, added light meter, metal slit shutter -/1000 sec. KKK No. KWE1600
$85 (B)

Nikon F3 AF
1982 small SLR camera with autofocus integrated into case via special prism, Nikkor adjustable lens 2.8/80 mm AF, slit shutter -/2000. KKK No. NIN0610
$750 (B)

Olympus FTL
1971-72 small SLR camera with TTL light meter, slit shutter 1-1/1000 sec., Zuiko adjustable lens 1.8/50 mm. KKK No. OLY0680
$80 (B)

Ihagee Exakta VX 500
1969 small SLR camera with Jena T adjustable lens 2.8/50 mm, slit shutter -/30 - -/500 sec. KKK No. IHA2440
$60 (B)

Asahi Pentax Asahiflex I
1952 small SLR camera with Takumar adjustable lens 3.5/50 mm, light shaft, slit shutter 1/25-1/500 sec. KKK No. ASA0030
$425

MINIATURE CAMERAS

Wirgin Edixa 16 M
1967-69 minicamera 12 x 17 mm,
Xenar 2.8/25 mm, selenium light
meter, automatic shutter 1/30-1/125
sec. KKK No. WIR0350
$80

Junka
1935 minicamera, 3 x 4 cm, for roll film,
Achromat 8.0/45 mm, simple shutter, optical
viewfinder. KKK No. JUK0030
$50

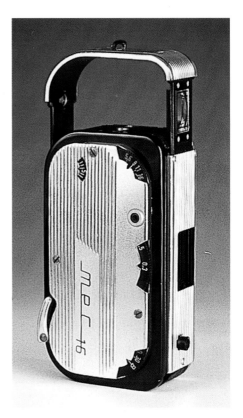

Feinwerktechnik MEC 16
1956 minicamera, 10 x 14 mm, sliding
viewfinder, Color-Ennit 2.8/20 mm, shutter 1/
30-1/1000 sec. KKK No. FEW0010
$100

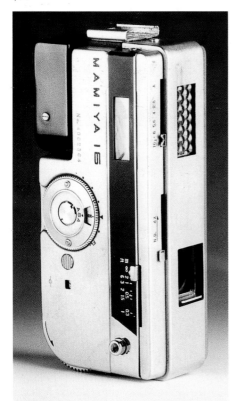

Mamiya 16
1950 minicamera, 10 x 14 mm, Sekor 2.8/25
mm, folding viewfinder. KKK No.
MAM0160
$85

Rollei A 110
1974-78 pocket camera, 13 x 17 mm, for 110 film, Tessar 2.8/23 mm, automatic flash. KKK No. ROL0610
$90

Kodak Pocket-Instamatic 400
1972-75 pocket camera, 13 x 17 mm, for 110 film, automatic flash with CdS cell, blue release. KKK No. KOD5720
$15

Rollei 16
1963-64 minicamera, 12 x 17 mm, Tessar 2.8/25 mm, selenium light meter, shutter 1/30-1/500 sec. KKK No. ROL0160
$110

Wirgin Edixa 16 MB
1969-73 minicamera 12 x 17 mm, coupled light meter, Xenar 2.8/25 mm, shutter 1/30-1/125 sec. KKK No. WIR0360
$90

Agfamatic 4000 Flash Pocket
1976 pocket camera, 13 x 17 mm, for 110
film, Color-Apotar 6.5/27 mm, light setting
via symbols, built-in electronic flash. KKK
No. AGF0580
$40

Agfa Snapper blue
1982 pocket camera, 13 x 17 mm, for 110
film, sensor release, blue plastic case, also
made in green, gray, red, and silver. KKK No.
AGF3060
$20

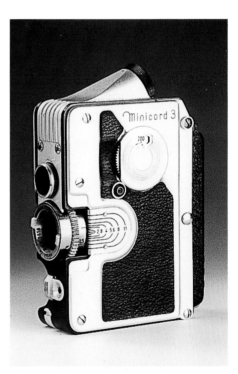

Brinkert Efbe
ca. 1960 minicamera for round film discs, 9 x
12 mm format, simple shutter, Color-Ennit
2.8/20 mm, unique design by Franz Brinkert
(F.B.) of Duisburg. KKK No. BRI0030
$70

Goerz Minicord 3
1958 minicamera, TLR 10 x 14, shaped like a
narrow film camera, Goerz Helgor 2.0/25
mm, shutter 1/10-1/400 sec. KKK No.
GOW0030
$230

Goldammer Goldeck 16
1959 minicamera, 10 x 14 mm, for 16 mm
film, Color-Ennit adjustable lens 2.8/20 mm,
Vario-Prontor shutter. KKK No. GOL0090
$125

Juka
1950 minicamera, 3 x 4 cm, for roll film,
Achromat 8.0/45 mm, simple shutter, optical
viewfinder. KKK No. JUK0040
Value estimate not possible

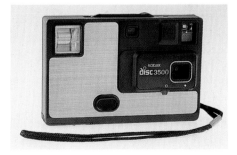

Kodak Mini-Instamatic S40
1976-78 pocket camera, 13 x 17 mm, for 110
film, Reomar 5.6/25 mm, automatic flash via
electronic shutter. KKK No. KOD5200
$30

Kodak Disc 3500
1983-84 disc camera, 8 x 10.5 mm, Fixfokus
lens 2.8/12.5 mm, built-in electronic flash,
bronze-colored case front, motorized film
advance. KKK No. KOD1890
$15

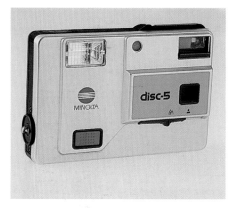

Minolta Disc 5
1983 disc camera, 8 x 10.5 mm, Minolta lens
2.8/12.5 mm, built-in electronic flash,
motorized film advance, shutter 1/100 and 1/
200. KKK No. MIN1490
$40

Meopta Mikroma II
1957 minicamera, 10.5 x 11.5 cm, for 16 mm
film, Mirar 3.5/20 mm, shutter -/400 sec.
KKK No. MEO0320
$100

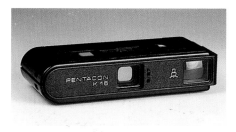

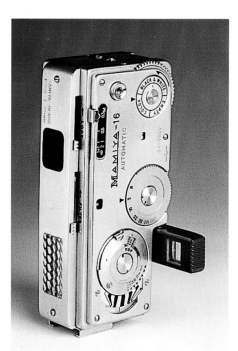

KW Pentcon K 16
1987 minicamera, 13 x 17 mm, for special
film with central perforation, Fixfokus lens
8.0/27 mm, controls with symbols. KKK No.
PEN0010
$40

Mamiya 16 Automatic
1960 minicamera, 10 x 14 mm, Sekor 2.8/25
mm, built-in selenium light meter. KKK No.
MAM0180
$85

Kalos
1950 minicamera, 9 x 12 mm, Mikro-
Anastigmat 4.5/20 mm, shutter 1/30-1/100
sec. KKK No. KAO0010
$750

Isoplast Fips
1954 minicamera, 13 x 13 mm, for 16 mm
film, Bakelite case, Achromat 6.5/25 mm.
KKK No. ISP0030
$100

Frica
Date unknown, minicamera, 10 x 14 mm,
semicircular Bakelite case, very rare, probably
German or French origin. KKK No. FCA0010
$450

Minox Riga
1938-40 minicamera, 8 x 11 mm, for Minox
film, Minostigmat 3.5/15 mm, shutter 1/2-1/
1000 sec. KKK No. MIX0010
$800

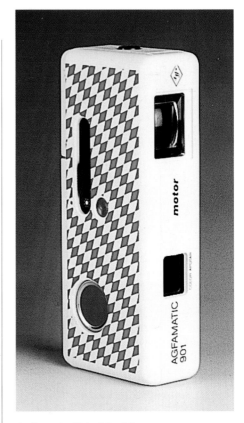

Minolta 16 MG-5
1970 minicamera, 12 x 17 mm, for 16 mm film, Rokkor 3.5 or 2.8/23 mm, shutter 1/30-1/500 sec, automatic flash. KKK No. MIN0890
$60

Agfamatic 901 white-blue
1979 pocket camera, 13 x 17 mm, for 110 film, special "Bayern" (Bavaria) series, motorized film advance, Apotar 8.0/27 mm, KKK No. AGF0270
$125

Minox 110 S
1977 minicamera, 13 x 17 mm, for 110 pocket film, four-lensed lens 2.8/25 mm, automatic flash, mixing rangefinder. KKK No. MIX0270
$75

Agfamatic 4008
1978 minicamera, 13 x 17 mm, for 110 film, Apotar 6.5/27 mm, electric shutter with automatic flash, 30-1/500 sec. KKK No. AGF0590
$25

Yashica Atoron Electro
1970 minicamera, 8 x 11 mm, for Minox film,
Yashinon 2.8/18 mm, automatic flash via CdS
cell, shutter 8-1/350 sec. KKK No. YAS0540
$75

Pentax Auto 110
1979 minicamera, 13 x 17 mm, for 110 film,
Standardobjektiv adjustable lens 2.8/18 mm,
automatic flash, settable winder. KKK No.
ASA0090
$140

Nikoh Minimax Lite/Minimax
1980-82 minicamera, 8 x 11 mm, for Minox
film, Suzunon 3.8/14.3 mm, or Fixfokus; at
left is Minimax Lite with built-in cigarette
lighter. KKK No. NIG0030 or 0020
$50; $40

Kiev 303 black
1990 minicamera, 13 x 17 mm, for 16 mm
film, Industar 3.5/23 mm, shutter 1/30-1/250
sec., case slides together. KKK No. KIV0250
$30

Voigtländer Vitoret 110
1976-78 minicamera for 110 pocket film,
·Lanthar 5.6/24 mm Fixfokus, shutter 1/60 and
1/125 sec. KKK No. VOL2310
$45

Kunik "Mickey"
1958 minicamera, 14 x 14 mm, for special roll
film, red case, Meniskus 9/25 mm, rare, not
authorized by Disney. KKK No. KUK0015
$130

Sida Standard
1938 minicamera with massive black-painted
cast case, Sida lens 8/35, simple shutter. KKK
No. SID0110
$40

STEREO CAMERAS

Meopta Mikroma Stereo 1 green
1962 minicamera, 10.5 x 11.5 mm,
Mirar 3.5/25 mm, Synchro shutter -/
100, green leather finish. KKK No.
MEO0360
$190

Contessa-Nettel Stereax
1912-19 stereo folding folding camera, 45 x
107 mm, Rietzschel Dialyt 6.8/60 mm, slit
shutter 1/5-1/1200, plate magazine. KKK No.
CNT0750
$250

Rietzschel Cosmo-Clack
1914-25 stereo-panorama camera, 45 x 107
mm, Stereo-Compur -/250, Rietzschel Linear-
Anast. 4.5/65 mm. KKK No. RIE0200
$250

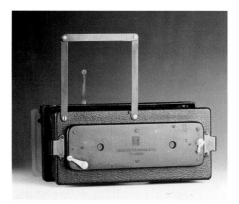

Ernemann Lilliput Stereo
1914-25 stereo folding folding camera for 45
x 107 mm plates, Achromat, simple shutter.
KKK No. ERN2570
$200

Altissa Errtee Stereo
1933 stereo box, 6 x 13 cm, leathered wood,
Duplar 1:11, simple shutter. KKK No.
ALT0440
$170

Wray Stereo-Graphic
1950 small stereo camera, 24 x 22 mm, Wray lens 4.0/35 mm, simple shutter, made under Graflex license. KKK No. WRY0020
$145

Wirgin Edixa Stereo III
1957 small stereo camera, 24 x 24 mm, Cassar 3.5/35 mm, Prontor -/300, selenium light meter. KKK No. WIR1430.
$175

Rollei Heidoskop 45 x 107 mm
1921-41 stereo box with changeable magazine, 45 x 107 mm, Tessar 4.5/55 mm, Stereo-V 1-/300, central viewfinder lens. KKK No. ROL0020
$375

GOMZ Sputnik
1960 Bakelite stereo camera, 6 x 13 cm,
Industar T-22 4.5/75 mm, -/15-/125, reflex
viewfinder with light shaft. KKK No.
GMZ0540
$190

Voigtländer Stereoflektoskop
1913-47 stereo camera, 45 x 107 mm, with
changeable magazine, Heliar 4.5/60 mm,
Compur -/250. KKK No. VOL1360
$325

Belca Belplasca
1954-62 stereo camera, 24 x
30 mm, Tessar 3.5/37/5 mm,
shutter 1-1/200 sec., about
5000 were made. KKK No.
BEL0060
$350

SPECIAL CAMERAS

Finetta Bolsey 8
1958 minicamera, 8 x 8 mm, for
single and film photography, with
built-in spring drive, Finon 2.8/7/5
mm, rotating shutter, rare. KKK No.
FIN0010
$200

Nikon Nikonos II

1968 small underwater camera with Nikkor-W adjustable lens 3.5/35 mm, capable of diving to 50 meters, shutter to 1/500 sec. KKK No. NIN1350
$250

Suzuki Opt. Co. Camera Lite

1950 minicamera, 5 x 8 mm, built into lighter, Echor 3.5/15 mm, simple shutter, rare. KKK No. SUZ0020
$350

Noble Noblex Pro 6/150 F

1993 panoramic camera, 6 x 12 cm, for 120 roll film, with electric motor-driven pivoting Tessar lens 4.5/50 mm, distance settings 1 meter, 5 meters, and infinity, SV -/30-/250. KKK No. NOB0020
$2300

Krasnogorsk Horizont

1967-73 small panoramic camera, 24 x 58 mm, mechanically driven pivoting OF-28 P lens, 2.8/28 mm, V: -/2-/250, sold with Cyrillic and Latin lettering. KKK No. KRA0100
$25

KGB F-21
1980 small camera, 18 x 24 mm, with built-in spring motor, lens 2.0/28 mm, made in Krasnogorsk for Soviet secret service. KKK No. KGB0020
$625

Nimslo Ltd. Nimslo 3D Camera
1980 small 3D camera with four lenses for three-dimensional photos on color negative film, Quadra lens 5.6/40 mm (4x), program shutter. KKK No. NIM0010
$110

Kodak EK8
1977-79 instant camera, 68 x 91 mm, with motorized photo ejector, folding case, distance setting, Kodak lens 11/137 mm, program shutter -/20/300. KKK No. KOD2210
$40

GOMZ Moment
1953 instant camera, 8 x 10.5 cm, for separate picture process, T-26 lens 6.8/135 mm, ZV / 10-/200, copy of Polaroid 95. KKK No. GMZ0270
$150

Secam Stylophot Standard
1955 minicamera, 10 x 10 mm for 16 mm film, in the shape of a pen, Achromat 6.3/27 mm, simple shutter. KKK No. SEC0010
$100

Secam Stylophot de Luxe
1956 minicamera, 10 x 10 mm for 16 mm film, in the shape of a pen, Roussel Anastigmat 3.5/27 mm, simple shutter. KKK No. SEC0020
$125

Nikon F Highspeed
1972 special model of the Nikon F with rigid mirror, thus maximum photo frequency of 7 per second with rigid motor drive.
Rare, no value estimate possible

Stirn Concealec Vest No. 1
1886 metal camera for round discs, 6 photos per film, periscope lens 10/42 mm, rotating shutter -/30 sec, rare. KKK No. STN0010
$865